LIVING IN...
ANCIENT MESOPOTAMIA

LIVING IN...
ANCIENT
MESOPOTAMIA

Series consultant editor: Norman Bancroft Hunt

CHELSEA HOUSE
PUBLISHERS

An imprint of Infobase Publishing

LIVING IN ANCIENT MESOPOTAMIA

Text and design © 2009 Thalamus Publishing

Chelsea House
An imprint of Infobase Publishing
132 West 31st Street
New York, NY 10001

Library of Congress Cataloging-in-Publication Data

Bancroft-Hunt, Norman.
  Living in Ancient Mesopotamia / Norman Bancroft Hunt. — 1st ed.
      p. cm. — (Living in the ancient world)
  Includes index.
  ISBN 978-0-8160-6337-6
  1. Iraq—History—To 634. 2. Iraq—Social life and customs. 3. Iraq—Religious life and customs. I. Title. II. Series.

  DS71.B36 2008
  935—dc22

                          2008005265

Chelsea House books are available at special discounts when purchased in bulk quantities for businesses, associations, institutions or sales promotions. Please call our Special Sales Department in New York at (212) 967-8800 or (800) 322-8755.

You can find Chelsea House Publishers on the World Wide Web at http://www.chelseahouse.com

For Thalamus Publishing
Series consultant editor: Norman Bancroft Hunt
Project editor: Warren Lapworth
Maps and design: Roger Kean

Printed and bound in China

10 9 8 7 6 5 4 3 2 1
This book is printed on acid-free paper

Picture acknowledgments
All illustrations by Oliver Frey except for – Jean-Claude Golvin: 10–11; John James/Temple Art: 18–19, 32–33; Roger Kean: 12–13 (all), 35 (center); Mike White/Temple Art: 60, 61 (top and bottom), 68–69, 74, 86–87 (main), 88–89.

Photographs – Paul Almasy/Corbis: 83; Archivo Iconografica/Corbis: 20, 39, 40, 68, 74 (left), 74 (right), 76; Bettman/Corbis: 35; Gianni Dagli Orti/Corbis: 25, 36 (Bottom), 37, 39, 46, 46 (Inset), 50, 53, 62, 63, 72 (both), 79; David Lees/Corbis: 36 (top), 55; Francis G. Mayer/Coris: 40 (top); Sandro Vannini/Corbis: 93; Thalamus Publishing: 45, 73; Nik Wheeler/Corbis: 14.

CONTENTS

Place in History

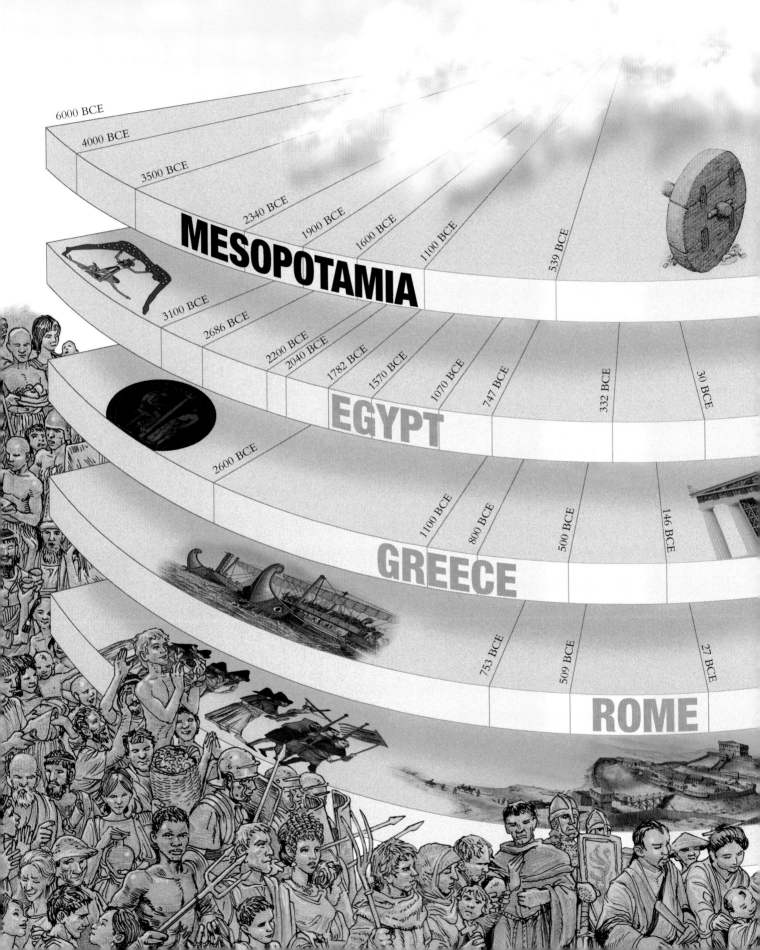

6000 BCE
4000 BCE
3500 BCE
2340 BCE
1900 BCE
1600 BCE
1100 BCE
539 BCE

MESOPOTAMIA

3100 BCE
2686 BCE
2200 BCE
2040 BCE
1782 BCE
1570 BCE
1070 BCE
747 BCE
332 BCE
30 BCE

EGYPT

2600 BCE
1100 BCE
800 BCE
500 BCE
146 BCE

GREECE

753 BCE
509 BCE
27 BCE

ROME

476 CE

800 CE

1200 CE

1350 CE

1450 CE

MIDDLE AGES

What Mesopotamia Did for Us

Mesopotamia's place in history is unique. It was here that, in the Western world, primitive humans became the first farmers, the first town dwellers, and the creators of urban civilization. In Mesopotamia were discovered the secrets of fire, of bronze, and of the wheel. Literature began with the development of a universal writing system. Science began its first halting steps with simple and then ever more sophisticated mathematics. It was in Mesopotamia that kings evolved a code of common law on which much of history would depend. No wonder, then, that Mesopotamia is called the "Cradle of Civilization."

Landscape and Climate

Mesopotamia means "between the rivers," and is the name given to the narrow strip of land between the Tigris and Euphrates rivers. Mesopotamia forms the larger part of what historians call the "Fertile Crescent."

The Fertile Crescent is a semicircle of land stretching from the southeast coast of the Mediterranean Sea, around the Syrian Desert north of Arabia, to the Persian Gulf.

The ancient region of Mesopotamia covered what today is the north of Syria, the southeast of Turkey, most of central Iraq, and a small part of western Iran. The northern areas are dominated by steep hills through which the Euphrates and Tigris flow in deep channels. The southern region is a mix of marshy plain and desert.

Throughout Mesopotamia, the typical climate consists of hot summers and relatively cold winters. Rainfall occurs in the winter and spring, but it is unevenly distributed and concentrated mostly on the northern rim. For this reason, only Upper Mesopotamia—the northern region—can support crops fed by rainfall. In the remainder, farming is dependent on the flood plains of the Euphrates, Tigris, and their tributaries. The ancient farmers also used irrigation canals running between the rivers. Only nomadic tribesmen lived in the northern central plain between the two rivers and beyond the rivers' valleys.

A changing coastline

Although the climate has remained relatively unchanged over 10,000 years, the course of the rivers in the southern plain has altered many times. Since the ancients relied on having a supply of water nearby, any towns along its banks had to be abandoned whenever the river changed its course. The two rivers carry a great deal of silt from the Turkish and Armenian Mountains, and over the years this has built up in the Persian Gulf. As a result the Gulf's coastline has changed greatly from ancient times and today this has left ports such as Ur more than 150 miles inland.

The first farmers migrated from the Zagros Mountains by 6000 BCE, where they had learned to cultivate the wild wheat that grew in the rainy hills. They began to dig trenches to irrigate the plain, and began making settlements. They were the Sumerians, and this is when our story begins, on page 14.

1. Khorramshahr
2. Abadan
3. Khosrowabad
4. Al Faw
5. Mah Shahr

6. River Karun
7. Shatt al Arab (combined flow of Euphrates and Tigris)
8. Bubiyan (island belongs to Kuwait)
9. Persian Gulf

8

The far south of Mesopotamia seen from space

A Brief History of Mesopotamia, 6000–539 BCE

Over a period of almost 5500 years, many different types of people inhabited ancient Mesopotamia. What we know about them comes from archaeological excavations.

The archaeologist's task is not an easy one—piecing together the lives of long-dead races from the remains of their civilization. In Mesopotamia, history comes in vertical slices, cut through the numerous *tells* that abound throughout the region. *Tell* is the technical term given to the large mounds created by thousands of years of building on the same spot.

Because the bricks were made of mud allowed to dry out under the baking sun, they crumbled easily. This meant that they could not be reused in the building of a new house, and so the builders just knocked them into a pile to make a foundation for the next building on top. In this way, over time, the settlements rose well above the level of the plain as large mounds.

Sumerian inventors

The first civilization is known as 'Ubaid, after Tell-al-'Ubaid, where distinctive types of pottery were first discovered. The 'Ubaid culture spread all across southern and central Mesopotamia, and the first temples were begun. The 'Ubaid Period was followed by the Sumerians in about 3500 BCE.

The people of Sumer spoke a language unrelated to any other, and we do not know exactly where they came from before appearing in Mesopotamia, though it was most likely some region of Asia. But they were not a unified race, preferring to make independent settlements, each with its own ruler, and they often made war on each other.

The Sumerians prospered, and their original small villages grew into large urban centers, such as Ur, the most famous city of its time. They built even bigger temples to the various Mesopotamian gods, and are famed for the discovery of many sciences we take for granted today, such as the wheel, an alphabet and writing system, and mathematics.

Sumer's neighbor to the east was the Iranian land of Elam. To the north dwelt many mountain peoples, collectively known as the Guti. Adjoining Sumer in a westerly semicircle were the Semites. They were an extension of the inhabitants of Palestine and Canaan, known in Mesopotamia as the Akkadians, after their capital city of Agade. Later on they become distinguished in the south as Babylonians and in the north as Assyrians.

In 2340 BCE, the Akkadians caused the fall of the Sumerian city-states, but in all the events that followed, the Sumerians never disappeared. Their culture simply became a part of the conquerors' societies, and Sumerian influence continued to be felt throughout the subsequent eras.

The first Mesopotamian empire

The Akkadians were led by King Sargon in 2335–2279 BCE. He is often called the first empire builder, because he united all the warring Sumerian city-states under his banner. His empire stretched all the way from the Persian Gulf to the Mediterranean in what is today Lebanon.

In 2230 BCE, the Guti swept out of the Zagros Mountains and took control of Sumeria for 120 years. The Sumerian kings regained their independence between 2109 and 2000 BCE, but then declined and fell prey to the Elamites. In time, these Elamites merged with the Sumerians.

Babylon becomes a power

From 1900 BCE, the city of Babylon grew in power, and in 1763, the Babylonian King Hammurabi extended his influence throughout Mesopotamia. He was first of a long line of kings that ruled what is called Old Babylonia for 300 years. Babylonia adopted Sumerian writing and counting systems, and developed geometry, algebra, calculus and logarithmic tables.

Babylonia's administrative system was so efficient that it influenced every empire that followed it—although the state was not left

Representing the early era, this female tomb figure of c.5000 BCE is a pre-Sumerian "mother goddess." Representing the later period, the city of Babylon at its peak: the Hanging Gardens (*pages 86–87*) dominate the Euphrates and the royal palace beyond and to the right. The blue-colored arch in the center is the famous Ishtar Gate (*pages 88–89*). The Tower of Babel is off the picture to the right.

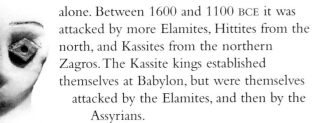

alone. Between 1600 and 1100 BCE it was attacked by more Elamites, Hittites from the north, and Kassites from the northern Zagros. The Kassite kings established themselves at Babylon, but were themselves attacked by the Elamites, and then by the Assyrians.

Under its powerful kings, Assyria grew from 1400 to its maximum extent in 680 BCE, dominating all of Mesopotamia and much of the Mediterranean coast, until it too fell to a new foe—the Persian Medes. Our story ends with them, their Tower of Babel, and their famous King Nebuchadnezzar II. His was a short-lived empire—between 605–562 BCE—and his weak successors were unable to prevent the disintegration of the state. It fell to the Achaemenid Persians (the enemies of ancient Greece), who were followed by the Arsacid Parthian dynasty (foes of the Roman Empire) and their successors, the Sassanian Persians. A brief account of their history may be found on pages 92–93.

Queen of cities

The reconstruction below shows Babylon at its height, during Nebuchadnezzar's reign (605–562 BCE). The city is capital of a vast empire, including the entirety of Mesopotamia, that rivals that of Egypt.

Covering an area of some 2470 acres, Babylon figures in its time as the largest on earth. Its outermost wall encloses an area of over 4.5 square miles, in the center of which rises the heart of the city—a rectangle spanning almost 2 miles on the longest side and by 1.25 miles on the other.

This center consists of two unequal parts, split by the Euphrates and connected by a bridge. To the west lies the New City, protected by double walls; to the east a triple-walled defense protects the more important zone known as the Old Quarter, essentially composed of the royal palace complex, palatial residences and religious cult monuments.

Table of Major Dates

All dates BCE	7000	5000	4000	3000	2500
PEOPLE AND CULTURE	• Ice Age ends • First permanent settlement at Qal'at Jarmo (near Kirkuk) in mountain foothills • Northern farmers leave rainbelt to settle in the plains, c.6000 • Simple pottery in common usage	• 'Ubaid style pottery starts appearing • Beginning of irrigation along river banks • Plow invented drawn by cattle, c.4500	• Widespread trade along rivers and canals facilitates rise of bigger temples and cities • Wheel invented, c.3500 • Simple bronze tools in use, c.3250	• Sumerians develop cuneiform writing • Construction of the Royal Tombs of Ur, 2600, excavated by Leonard Woolley in the 20th century	• King Ur-Nammu writes his law code, c.2050 • Domesticated horses are used, c.2000 *Impression from a cylinder seal.*

Early bronze sickle with wooden handle.

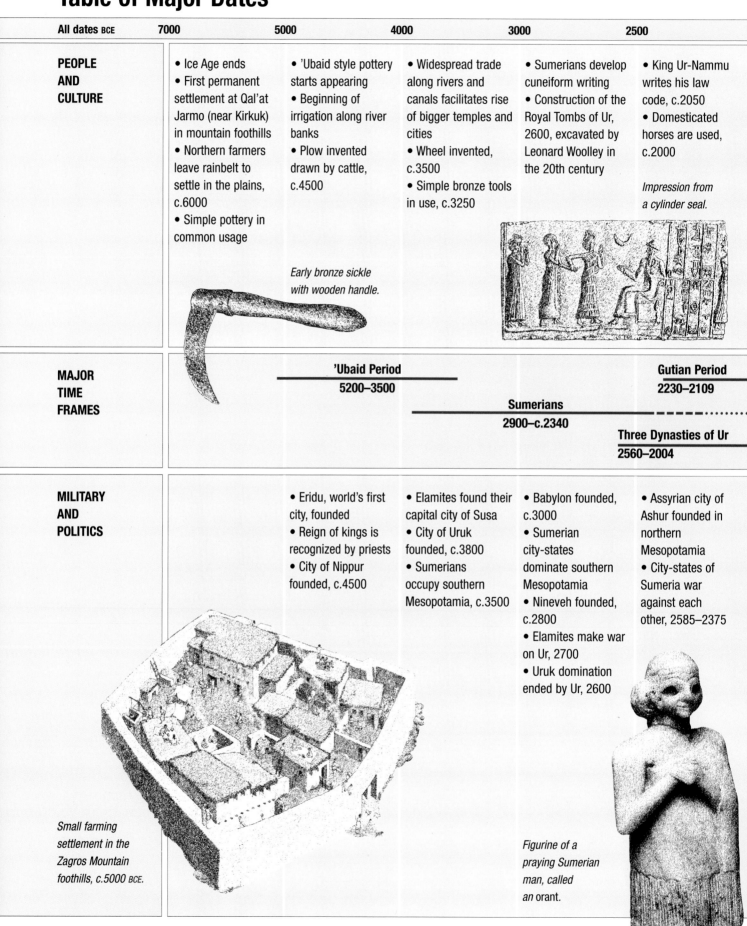

MAJOR TIME FRAMES		**'Ubaid Period** **5200–3500**		**Sumerians** **2900–c.2340**	**Gutian Period** **2230–2109** **Three Dynasties of Ur** **2560–2004**

| **MILITARY AND POLITICS** | | • Eridu, world's first city, founded
• Reign of kings is recognized by priests
• City of Nippur founded, c.4500 | • Elamites found their capital city of Susa
• City of Uruk founded, c.3800
• Sumerians occupy southern Mesopotamia, c.3500 | • Babylon founded, c.3000
• Sumerian city-states dominate southern Mesopotamia
• Nineveh founded, c.2800
• Elamites make war on Ur, 2700
• Uruk domination ended by Ur, 2600 | • Assyrian city of Ashur founded in northern Mesopotamia
• City-states of Sumeria war against each other, 2585–2375 |

Small farming settlement in the Zagros Mountain foothills, c.5000 BCE.

Figurine of a praying Sumerian man, called an orant.

2000	1500	1000	800	700	600	500

• Texts begin to detail science, diplomacy, and religion as well as administration
• Domesticated horses begin to be used for pulling carts
• Mari established as key point on trading route between Syria and Mesopotamia
• Code of Hammurabi of Babylon formulated
• Abraham leaves Ur, travels to Israel, c.1900–1750

• Hittites become first culture to smelt iron, 1500
• First real "alphabet" is employed at Ugarit

• Ashurnasirpal's great palace is built at Nimrud

Temple at Uruk

• Dur-Sharrukin is constructed as Assyrian capital of Sargon II, but never completed, 720–705

• King Ashurbanipal builds his Library at Nineveh, c.650, and collects works from the "known world"
• Birth of Zarathustra, founder of the Zoroastrian religion, c.628

• Nebuchadnezzar II builds the Hanging Gardens and completes the ziggurat of Etemenanki (Tower of Babel), c.590–560

Gold necklace of leaves

Old Babylonia
1900–1100

Hittite invasions
1600–1300

Mittani invasions
1500–1275

Assyrian Empire
1429–609

• Royal dynasty founded at Babylon, 1900
• Assyrian rulers of Ashur, Nineveh, and Arbel unite, 1800
• Hittites establish capital of Hattusas in Turkey, 1750
• Hittites invade Babylonia, 1595

• Egyptians under Thutmose III war against Hittites, 1460
• Assyria becomes independent of Hittites, 1365
• Battle of Kadesh between Egyptians and Hittites, 1275. Both sides claim victory
• Egypt makes peace with Hittites, 1272
• Shalmaneser I founds Nimrud, 1250
• Kassites drive Elamites out of Babylon and Assyrians begin southward expansion, 1185
• Tilgath-Pileser confirms Assyrian rule of Babylon, 1100

• Chaldeans invade city of Ur, c.900
• Nimrud becomes Assyrian capital, c.870

• Tilgath-Pileser III declares himself king of Assyria and Babylon, 729
• The Ten Tribes of Israel expelled from Palestine by King Sargon II, 722
• Carchemish, last Hittite stronghold, falls to Assyria, 717

• Assyrian king Sennacherib destroys Babylon, 689
• Assyria conquers Egypt, 671
• Medes make Persia a vassal state, 640
• Nabopolassar, Assyrian governor of Babylon, makes himself king of the new Chaldean empire, 626
• Nabopolassar defeats Assyrians in two battles, 616
• Assyrians make Harran their capital, 612, abandoned 609
• Nebuchadnezzar II succeeds his father Nabopolassar, 605

Cuneiform clay tablet

• Nabodinus, last of the Neo-Babylonian/ Chaldean dynasty is defeated by Persian King Cyrus II
• First Persian Empire of the Achaemenids, 539–330, finally overthrown by Alexander the Great of Macedon

CHAPTER 1

The Sumerians

Expanding onto the Plain

It is about 6000 BCE, and a major change in where people live is occurring as some northern farmers move out of the mountainous rain belt and onto the desert plain.

In the Zagros Mountains and their foothills the rainfall amounts to 12 inches a year—the minimum required to grow crops. Nearer to the Tigris there is very little or no rainfall, but the farmers have learned how to harness the river system by digging irrigation canals to water the fertile desert soil. As a result, even though there is insufficient rain, they will be able to raise more crops than was ever possible when they lived in the hills.

Soon, the isolated farming settlements grow into small towns. One of the earliest known is called Hassunah. Its larger houses consist of six rooms arranged around a courtyard. There are large jars for storing grain and domed bread ovens. Their pottery is already elegant in shape, decorated with simple patterns in brown (*see page 20*).

The beginnings of civilization

Further to the south lies Tell-es-Sawwan, right beside the Tigris, and to its east on the rim of the plain sits Choga Mami. Both of these villages, being later than Hassunah, are larger—perhaps a thousand people live here. The houses are bigger—some even have two floors. And the villages have defensive ditches and embankments because there is the constant danger of raids from other settlements.

In some cases there is evidence of cobbled streets, which indicates a primitive form of government, since civil authority is required to maintain shared areas of a township. These early streets generally lead into the village's center, where there is a large open space for public access and meetings. It also acts as a market place for the local farmers to sell their produce.

Kings and conquest

Interestingly, most of the decorated pottery and burials are located within these public spaces, rather than restricted to household areas, as has previously been the case. This indicates that the inhabitants have developed community rituals, and also an associated formal leadership—the first kings.

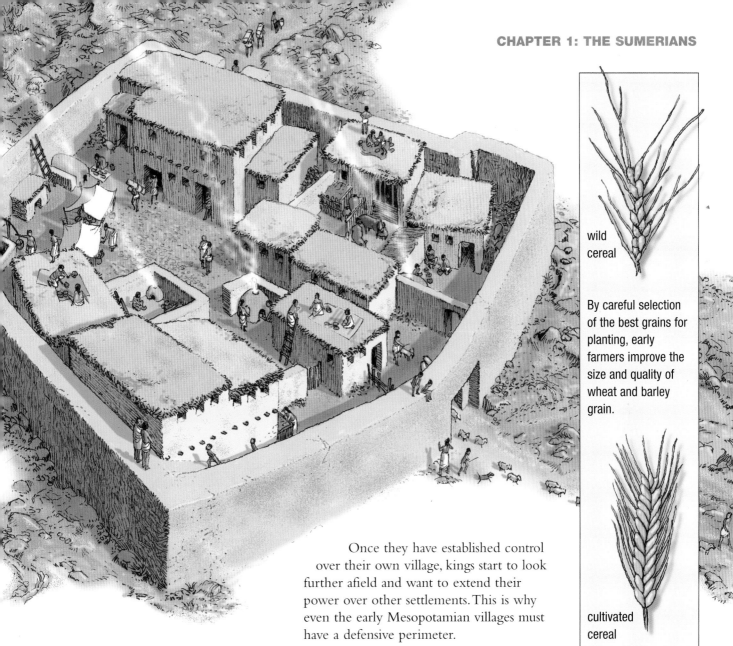

wild cereal

By careful selection of the best grains for planting, early farmers improve the size and quality of wheat and barley grain.

cultivated cereal

Once they have established control over their own village, kings start to look further afield and want to extend their power over other settlements. This is why even the early Mesopotamian villages must have a defensive perimeter.

Above: In the early morning the villagers go out through the defensive wall with their flocks of sheep and goats to grazing land. The settlement boasts a few two-story houses, an open meeting and market area, and paved street.

The illustration on the left shows the sharp contrasts of Mesopotamia—lush river-fed land, desert, and the distant, enclosing mountains.

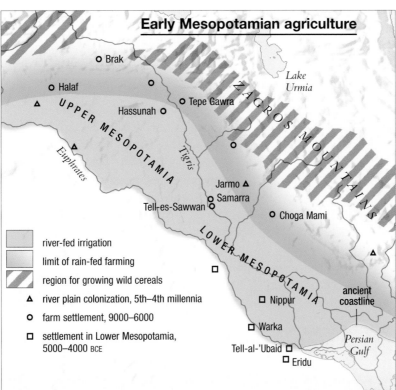

Early Mesopotamian agriculture

Brak

Halaf

Hassunah

Tepe Gawra

UPPER MESOPOTAMIA

Euphrates

Tigris

ZAGROS MOUNTAINS

Lake Urmia

Jarmo

Samarra

Tell-es-Sawwan

Choga Mami

LOWER MESOPOTAMIA

Nippur

Warka

Tell-al-'Ubaid

Eridu

ancient coastline

Persian Gulf

river-fed irrigation

limit of rain-fed farming

region for growing wild cereals

△ river plain colonization, 5th–4th millennia

○ farm settlement, 9000–6000

□ settlement in Lower Mesopotamia, 5000–4000 BCE

Over the years tamed wild sheep (top) have been bred to produce the smaller, docile domestic animal below.

15

Building Southern Mesopotamia

South of Tell-es-Sawwan, the primitive people of Lower Mesopotamia face a different problem with river water to their neighbors in the north—flooding.

The land in Lower Mesopotamia is more recent than in the mountainous north. The soil here has been built up over thousands of years by the silt brought down from the mountains of Armenia through the tireless activity of the Tigris and Euphrates rivers. Their silt is constantly adding to the land surface and cutting down the water area at the head of the Persian Gulf.

The first Sumerians to occupy this marshy basin are pioneers, engineers who must work hard to make the ground firm and suitable for the cultivation of crops. Fortunately, the Sumerians are helped by one plant that grows in natural abundance in waterlogged ground—marsh reeds.

Land reclamation scheme

As the labeled picture shows, some workers cut the reeds (**A**) and spread them out on ground at the edge of the marsh to dry out (**B**). When the reeds are almost dry, a second group weaves them into lengths of matting (**C**). These mats are then placed over the live reeds in the marsh and stamped down (**D**). Of course, the mats become soggy—but that is the point. As several layers of interlocking mats begin to rot into the live reeds beneath them, the marsh begins to stabilize.

Now the Sumerian farmers can begin to bring soil from the desert edges and throw it over the rotting reed mats (**E**). The process takes a very long time, but eventually entire regions of the rivers' banks are made firm. When the rivers flood, the extra silt is deposited over the reclaimed land, further adding to its fertility.

A baked clay sickle (right) and a bone-handled one with inset flint teeth for sawing are examples of tools early Mesopotamians use.

Giving thanks for the land

The cut reeds are also used for building the early dwellings and granaries of Sumer. Of one or two rooms, the thatched walls rise up into a curving roof. This is left open along the center to allow light into the hut. Because there is almost no rainfall, the Sumerians do not have to worry about getting the insides of their homes wet.

Close to the reclaimed land, the most important building is the cult hut (**F**). It is distinguished from domestic structures by the mud plastered on its outer walls. When this has dried out, patterns of religious significance are cut into the plastered surface.

A bundle of reeds tied near the top makes the two graceful curves that the Sumerians associate with the mother goddess, for this is her dwelling place. She is implored to protect the local Sumerians, their livestock, and crops from harm and disease. To honor her, the farmers make offerings of specially decorated pottery vessels, the most treasured items the early Sumerians possess.

Early Village Life

The early villages have developed from the original farming settlements. But as they grow larger, their inhabitants still depend on farming the land immediately around them.

Most people who live in this village are farmers, fishermen, or herders, but there are a few men who make pottery or manufacture weapons and utensils. A farmer must be capable of making and repairing his own tools, though he might pay for some help from a specialist in metalworking. No one has any money—coinage has not been invented yet—so farmers pay potters and metalsmiths for their services in kind, which means they agree on how much food the farmer will give the worker for his efforts.

Better housing

This small village, like almost all those in Sumer, clusters on the river bank. This is the source of water for drinking, bathing, and washing laundry. The early reed-thatched huts have been replaced by sturdier homes built from sun-dried mud bricks, which are then given a coating of mud plaster and painted with a mud-lime mixture. This dries to a white color, which reflects the harsh sunlight and helps to keep the interiors cool. The roofs are made from reed matting, as are the beehive-shaped granaries, barns, and animal stables.

New farming inventions

The farmers in this village can cultivate a lot of land because they have plows. The plow is pulled by two oxen with a driver walking behind to guide the plowshare and ensure its wooden blade digs into the soil. News has reached the villagers that a neighboring settlement has made a tremendous improvement by replacing the wooden blade with one made from the new metal called bronze (*see pages 24–25*).

For sowing, the farmer uses a new invention, an ox-drawn seed drill. This plants the seeds in rows instead of "broadcasting," or scattering the seed by hand. The plow-like device makes a furrow in the soil, and seeds in a wooden box trickle through a funnel and tube, then drop into the furrow.

Harnessing the river

Although the Tigris and Euphrates flood their banks each spring, for the rest of the year the sun bakes hard the reclaimed land. These farmers have learned how to build irrigation canals in order to store the river water and bring it to the fields. In this way, over the years, they have been able to plow and plant fields much further from the river than before.

With more land under cultivation, the village grows more food than it needs. It can sell this surplus to neighboring settlements. Having more food releases more people from farming to specialize in making useful goods—some men are given the permanent task of looking after the cult house and the mother goddess. They are the first priests.

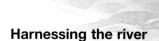

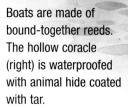

Boats are made of bound-together reeds. The hollow coracle (right) is waterproofed with animal hide coated with tar.

Crops grown

The main crops raised at this period are wheat and barley. A variety of vegetables (*see page 38*) is grown in smaller fields and local gardens, while the palms lining the rivers and canals provide dates. Domesticated sheep, goats, and cattle are reared, and the rivers give the people fish and wild waterfowl.

Invention of the Wheel, 3500–3250 BCE

After the discovery of fire in prehistoric times, no other development has made such an impact on humankind as the invention of the wheel. This magnificent device first appears here in Mesopotamia.

An old saying claims that "necessity is the mother of invention," and it is certainly true of the wheel. While the Sumerian farming settlements remain isolated, there is neither the need for trade nor the goods to sell. But our village has grown much larger, it is producing surplus food, and its potters can make more items than the village needs.

The potters and the farmers want to trade this surplus with other villages where different kinds of items are made. But their small reed boats are unstable when loaded and pack animals are both expensive and do not carry a sufficient weight for their cost.

An early 'Ubaid pottery vase of c.4500 BCE, typically decorated with brown-colored geometric patterning.

An 'Ubaid potter raises up a new vase on his wheel, turned by the apprentice's hands. Behind them, another potter loads the simple wood-fired kiln with dried pots, while greeting a passing trader on his wheeled cart.

From clay pots to wheeled carts

Meanwhile, the potters have been clever. They have discovered that they can make their pots more quickly by raising the clay vessels on a hand- or foot-operated turntable—a wheel. Not only is the process of "throwing" the clay faster, the resulting pots are much more accurately formed and elegant. We do not know who first recognized the benefit of adapting the potter's wheel for use in transport, but a wheeled vehicle pulled by two oxen can carry a greater weight of goods than the same number of pack animals.

Making a wheel

The solid wooden wheels are made from two or three lengths of plank cut to form a disk and fastened together with wooden or copper staples. Two wheels are then connected through their centers to an axle. Linchpins hammered through the end of the axle on either side of the wheel hold it in place, while allowing it to turn freely.

Four-wheeled carts are the most popular, though some villagers prefer the lighter two-wheeled version. The carts are drawn by one or more oxen, harnessed to the vehicle in a manner similar to that of the plow.

The 'Ubaid Period, c.5200–3500 BCE

The earliest permanent settlement of Lower Mesopotamia occurs some time before 5000, probably the consequence of non-Semitic tribes moving into the region. This marks the beginning of the 'Ubaid Period, which is named after the city of Tell-al-'Ubaid, where pottery with a distinctive type of geometric decoration is first made. But it is not restricted to the city: 'Ubaid pots may be found far to the south along the Persian Gulf coast, and it's made as far north as Tepe Gawra (*see the following pages*).

Right: A pack-drover watches enviously as heavily laden two- and four-wheeled wagons pass his mule, carrying as much as it can. The first wheels are simple creations (**below**) but they revolutionize trade. Lighter, spoked wheels will not be used until about 2000 BCE.

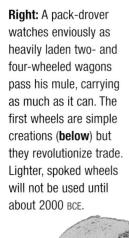

The wheel develops trade

The invention of the wheeled cart has speeded up trade and increased the distance it is possible to travel. Among the many types of goods carried in carts, few are as prized as 'Ubaid pots—for their fine decoration in naturalistic designs of plants, birds, fish, animals, and sometimes landscapes.

However, the commodity needed most by the village is copper ore for making metal objects, such as plow blades and knives. Fortunately, those settlements close to supplies of the raw ore are willing to trade some for the beautiful pottery vessels made in this village. How the copper ore is used is explained on pages 24–25.

The temple forecourt is a place of much community activity: a barber shaves a man's head to the tune of a boy's shin-bone pipe.

Above right: Villagers congregate for a religious ceremony, as the statue of a deity is pulled to the shrine's entrance on a sled.

Tepe Gawra—a Temple Through Time

While the Sumerian farmers in Lower Mesopotamia tame the river marshes and invent the plow, further north 'Ubaid civilization has reached a higher level of sophistication.

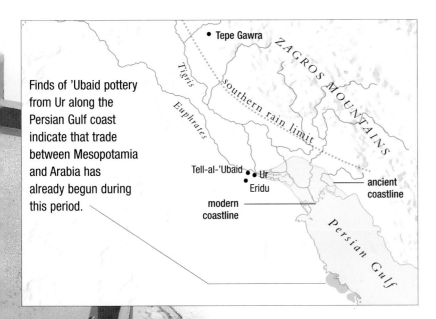

Finds of 'Ubaid pottery from Ur along the Persian Gulf coast indicate that trade between Mesopotamia and Arabia has already begun during this period.

The sacred precinct of Tepe Gawra, which lies 15 miles northeast of modern Mosul, Iraq, is typical of early Mesopotamian temples of the 'Ubaid Period. There are 26 layers of settlement sitting one on top of the other at Tepe Gawra, each one a little smaller in area than the preceding one. The most splendid period is found at Level 13, dating to approximately 3500 BCE.

Elegant shrines

The temple consists of three monumental shrines arranged in a U around a forecourt. As seen in the reconstruction, the nearest shrine is decorated with a vermilion coating, the central shrine is decorated with white plaster, while the one to the left retains the natural coloring of its sun-dried bricks.

Although the bricks used in each shrine are of different sizes, all three buildings use piers and pilasters (a half-column attached to the main wall), which create niches on the outside to enhance their visual appeal.

There are tombs surrounding the sacred precinct, some brick-built and some of cut stone, depending on the wealth of the families who own them. Three, in particular, indicate the great wealth of their owners, with grave goods of gold, electrum (an alloy of gold and silver), lapis lazuli gemstones, and ivory. These are all imported materials from the north and south of Mesopotamia, and indicate the advanced level of trading.

Manufacturing wealth

Pottery of the 'Ubaid style is made at Tepe Gawra, and it is traded far and wide because it is more reliable than the work from other places. This is because the potters here have discovered how to build closed kilns for firing the clay, which results in higher temperatures and therefore stronger vessels.

Other manufacturing at Tepe Gawra includes fine stone-cutting of objects ranging from sickle and weapon blades to engraved stamp seals (*see page 29*), and the craft of obsidian carving. Translucent obsidian is a volcanic stone that resembles glass when the raw block is gently ground down into a bowl or other container. Since it takes a lot of skill and patience to make one obsidian vessel, only the very rich can afford them.

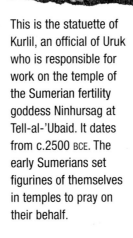

This is the statuette of Kurlil, an official of Uruk who is responsible for work on the temple of the Sumerian fertility goddess Ninhursag at Tell-al-'Ubaid. It dates from c.2500 BCE. The early Sumerians set figurines of themselves in temples to pray on their behalf.

The Bronze Age Begins, 3500 BCE

The rise of farming and town-dwelling has led to the possession of goods and a demand for more intricate and beautiful objects. The discovery of bronze revolutionizes Mesopotamia.

For more than a thousand years, the early Sumerians have been making objects by hammering lumps of raw copper ore, but this is a slow and laborious process. Many metalworkers now prefer the process of heating the ore to a high temperature in a container called a crucible—a process known as smelting. This makes the "slag" waste material separate from the pure copper, which is poured off and much easier to work with. While still hot the copper can be cast in pottery molds to form elegant shapes. The same is also done with gold and silver.

But far more exciting is the discovery of bronze. By using bellows to make the wood fire under the crucible burn even hotter, the imported copper is smelted together with imported tin. The resulting metal alloy is much stronger than copper alone.

The superiority of a bronze ax or sword is amply demonstrated when used against counterparts made from the traditional hammered copper or cut flint.

The traditional craft of hammering copper to create artifacts gives way to casting the molten metal in clay molds. The increased heat achieved by using bellows leads to the discovery of a tough new metal alloy, bronze.

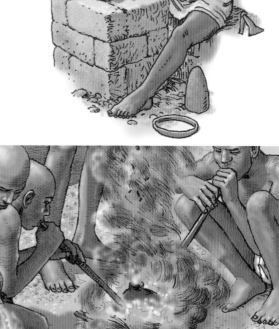

Tools, such as this sickle, benefit from bronze's greater strength.

Lost-wax casting

A rough shape is made in clay. Bronze pins are inserted (A) and a wax model is built around the core (B). The pins keep the clay core in place after the wax melts as the clay is fired. The wax model is covered by an outer clay mold (C). Molten bronze is poured into the gap left by the wax (D).

A

The growth of industry

The earlier farming village has now grown into a larger town inhabited by many specialist craftsmen, whose improving technology is transforming life. Each shares his discoveries with fellow craftsmen, and new inventions result. Thanks to the bronze metalworkers, Sumerian carpenters now have sharp, tough saws and drills to cut and shape their timber. Goldsmiths have learned the art of beating their metal into wafer-thin sheets and spinning it out into strands of super-fine filigree wire for jewelry.

Meanwhile, the smiths have discovered how to make bronze castings by the lost-wax method (*see the explanatory box below*). This involves making a model out of easily worked wax and then covering it with clay. When the clay is fired in a kiln, the wax melts and runs out, leaving a negative impression of the original model in the clay hollow. The clay mold is then filled with molten bronze and allowed to cool. Breaking apart the clay mold reveals the model in all its shining glory.

This superb bronze head shows the Sumerian metalworker's craft at its best. The fine detail is made possible by use of the lost-wax method of casting. Dating from about 2250 BCE, the head is thought to represent either of the Akkadian kings Sargon the Great or Naram-Sin (*see page 48*).

B C D

The outer clay mold is removed to reveal the finished figure. The "nib" on the head where the metal entered is then cut away.

The need to control supply

The power as well as the beauty of bronze is not lost on Sumer's neighbors when Sumerian merchants begin trading utensils, weapons, and armor. Obtaining materials for this new technique becomes literally a matter of life and death. Since the known sources of copper and tin are limited and widely scattered, control of the supply routes is essential. Everyone wants to monopolize the mines and supply routes—war will probably come soon.

Growth of the Town

Between 3500 and 2100 BCE, the Mesopotamian villages expand greatly into towns, and then cities. The populations swell from 5000 to as many as 30,000 at Uruk.

A council of elders runs a Sumerian town, but there is often war between the many expanding and competing urban centers. Sometimes it is over adjoining farm land, more often about who controls the copper and tin routes. When there is a war, the council appoints a wartime leader called a *lugal* (great man) to direct the military campaigns.

War drives more and more of the surrounding population into the town, which as a result has grown into a city of considerable size. Uruk—for a while the largest urban settlement in the world—covers an area of approximately 1200 acres, with a city wall of over 6 miles in length.

The frequent wars have also made it desirable to strengthen and raise the height of the defensive embankment. The wall has narrow entrance gates, while beyond the town's precincts are irrigated fields bisected by numerous canals to control the floodwaters of the Euphrates and Tigris.

Farmers either own or rent fields in which to plant their crops. They are responsible for ensuring that the canals are kept free of rushes and weeds, and officials are appointed to make sure they do so.

More officials weigh produce and issue receipts for cereals placed in the communal granaries. They also control affairs of state, as well as settling legal disputes and having the authority to determine appropriate punishment for wrongdoers.

The religious center

At the heart of Uruk is a complex of great temples. The most important are those of Eanna and Anu, each of which is in the form of a pyramid-shaped ziggurat. This is a new type of Sumerian temple that has grown high above other buildings by generations of rebuilding on the same site. It consists of a large brick-faced platform reached by a flight of steps. On top of the platform is a small building, or sanctuary, containing a shrine that is sacred to the god or goddess.

The kings of Ur

Not far from Uruk is another great city, Ur, in the process of becoming the dominant power in Lower Mesopotamia. Ur is almost constantly at war with its neighbors —Eridu, Lagash, Uruk, Larsa, Shuruppak, Nippur, and even as far north as mighty Kish.

For this reason the council of elders long ago appointed a permanent *lugal* to run the city and the army. His position has been confirmed as hereditary, so he may pass on the city's rule to his son—he is a king in every sense.

Reconstructions of the White Temple in the Sanctuary of Anu (**right**) and the Ziggurat of Uruk (**below**).

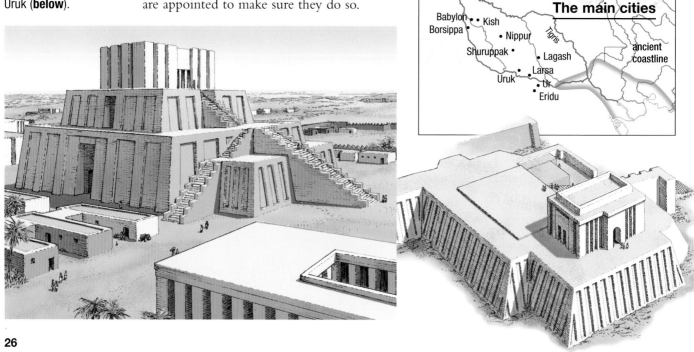

The main cities

Babylon
Borsippa
Kish
Nippur
Shuruppak
Lagash
Larsa
Uruk
Ur
Eridu
Tigris
ancient coastline

The benefits of war

War brings misery in its wake, since outlying farmers are killed in skirmishes and their inability to tend the land brings famine to city dwellers. But war also accelerates technological development—and the Sumerians are clever inventors. Ur's streets have become packed with the workshops of various artisans, each skilled in a particular type of armor and weapons manufacture. Many individual workers have already formed into co-operative groups, which can pool their skills and resources, making them more efficient.

In times of peace, these companies use the new techniques learned in the heat of war to make all the new luxury goods that the increasingly wealthy citizens demand.

The hustle and bustle of a typical town of Lower Mesopotamia in about 2500 BCE.

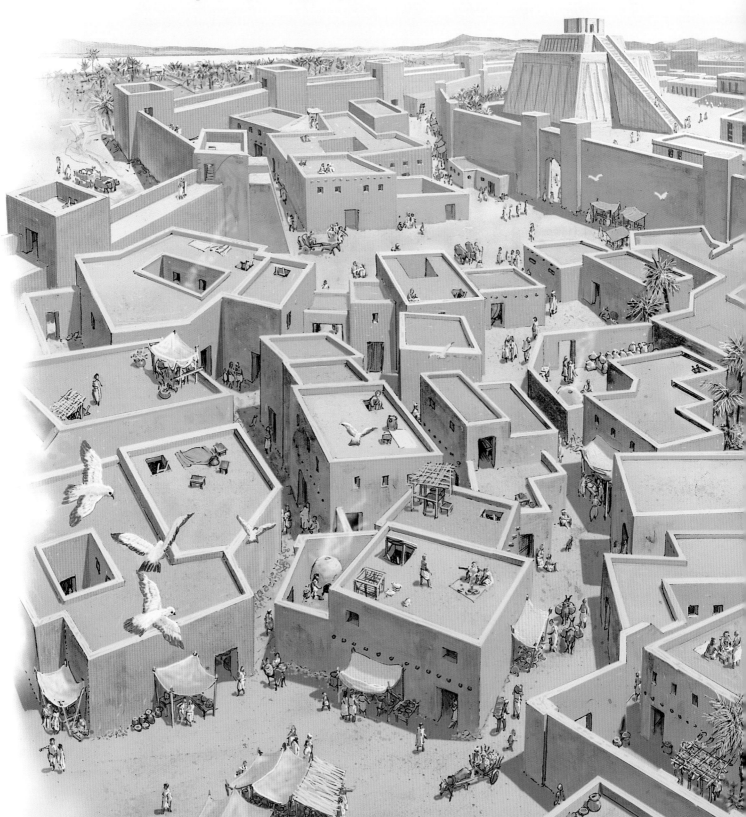

The Invention of Writing, 5000–2000 BCE

Clay stamps with an "ownership mark" are imposed by the court on an individual's property. They identify a person's wealth, and thus his responsibility in providing goods for temple upkeep. Ownership marks are the first form of writing.

According to the Sumerian epic poem of *Innana and Enki*, one hundred basic elements of civilization were passed from Eridu, City of the First Kings, to Uruk. Among these basic elements was writing. It's believed to be a divine decree from Enki, the God of Wisdom. Writing, therefore, is considered to be a gift of the gods, and it carries both power and knowledge—and of course knowledge *is* power.

However, the story of *Innana and Enki* is a myth—the art of writing has developed among the Sumerian people over a very long period. The use of earlier picture-symbols are shown on these two pages.

In a temple courtyard a seal cutter completes his newest piece, while a young apprentice rolls out a cylinder seal on clay to create a large pictogram. In the foreground another scribe writes with a stylus on a damp clay tablet.

Writing is used for keeping accounts, which help to organize the city's economy and administration. But some scholars are developing writing to describe more abstract ideas, such as religion and scientific matters. Perhaps most importantly, they are beginning to use writing to record events as they take place. This is the start of written history.

To do this they have begun to use the signs phonetically—that is, to indicate sounds rather than objects. In this way it is easy to build up many words. The scribes must memorize the Sumerian system's 600 signs; when combined in a different manner, signs are also used for arithmetic (*see pages 54–55*).

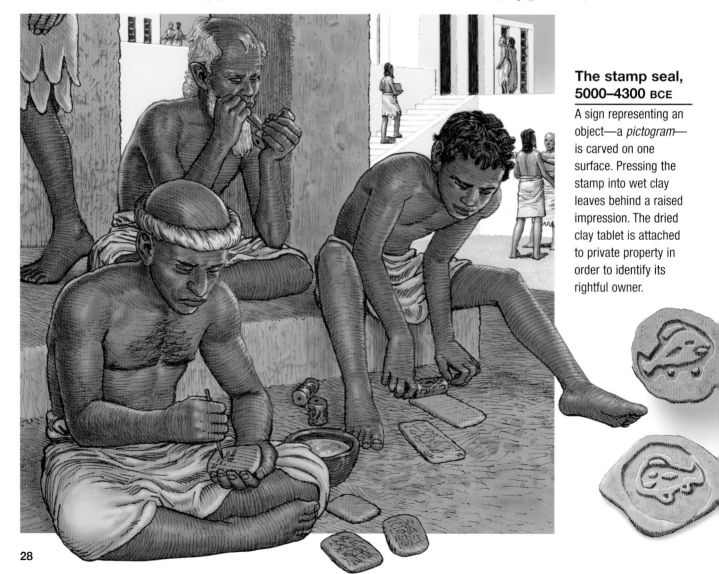

The stamp seal, 5000–4300 BCE

A sign representing an object—a *pictogram*—is carved on one surface. Pressing the stamp into wet clay leaves behind a raised impression. The dried clay tablet is attached to private property in order to identify its rightful owner.

The development of *cuneiform* script, 3100–2000 BCE

The earliest forms of *cuneiform* writing were *pictographic*—representations of familiar objects, such as a fish, an ox-head, and a bird, shown below in the first column. In time these were abstracted to representations of the objects (*second column*), written in vertical columns. In time people began writing horizontally to avoid smudging the marks as they wrote, and they rotated the symbols (*third column*). Eventually, further abstraction took place (*right column*).

For the last development a new type of stylus, or pen, came into use, which was pushed into the clay, producing wedge-shaped signs, known as *cuneiform* writing.

The Sumerian method of writing was adapted by Babylonia (*a sample shown on the top right*), Assyria, the Elamites, Kassites, Hittites, Mitanni, Hurrians, and Persians, developing into a complex system

of phonetics before yielding to the alphabet c.13th century BCE. At this time in the Syrian trading kingdom of Ugarit a 30–32 character *cuneiform* alphabet (*shown below*) was developed. It was later adapted by the Phoenicians and then the Greeks and Romans into the one we know today.

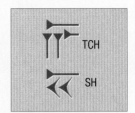

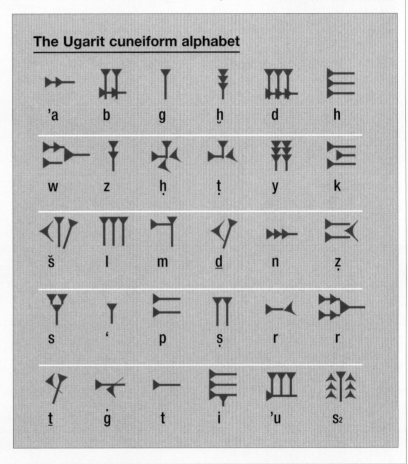

The Ugarit cuneiform alphabet

'a	b	g	ḫ	d	h
w	z	ḥ	ṭ	y	k
š	l	m	ḏ	n	ẓ
s	'	p	ṣ	r	r
ṯ	ġ	t	i	'u	s₂

Clay tablet counters, c.4500 BCE

This cone-shaped clay token bears an incised mark and serves as a counter in barter exchange. Sometimes the tokens are shaped to represent goods, as in the form of a cow's head, and further identified by scratched marks of ownership.

Cylinder seal, 4300 BCE

The cylinder seal allows for much more complex arrangements of pictograms. A stone cylinder is engraved with a series of pictographs, and when this is rolled over a rectangular tablet of wet clay it leaves behind a much longer impression. Cylinder seals are used mostly by the king, his ministers, and the temple priests.

A City Dwelling

Ringed by canal and embankment, Ur is built on a mound to prevent flooding. Its 24,000 inhabitants pack into houses on narrow, winding streets. Wealthy people live in large homes near the temple, but poorer citizens' houses are quite different.

In some respects, the slaves of nobles have a better quality of life than the poor free citizens. The single-story mud-brick houses of poor citizens are arranged along narrow unpaved roads or alleyways. These average about six feet in width, and they are too numerous to allow the cobblestone paving of the earlier, smaller villages.

Even in the poorer homes a separate area is kept aside to serve as a kitchen, with mud-brick ovens placed outside the rear of the building in a tiny courtyard. Because these houses have no plumbing, their occupants bathe in the river and most household waste is simply deposited into the alleyways.

Municipal workers are employed to keep the communal areas tidy, which usually means spreading a layer of ash and sand over the human waste. Over a period of time the accumulated waste, ash, and sand has increased the height of the roads, to the point that steps down to the houses are needed.

A puzzle of homes

Depending on their relative status and economic position, a family might possess only a single room or several for different functions, such as living, sleeping, or eating. Generally, the better off—especially artisans—use the room nearest to the street as a shop or workplace.

If a man's economic position improves, he can take over a room from the next-door house belonging to a poorer neighbor. In this way, the packed houses resemble a jigsaw puzzle of interlocking rooms, with new doors knocked through the adjoining walls and older doors blocked up, as each family's fortunes improve or worsen.

This plan shows the "jigsaw puzzle" layout of Sumerian homes. Each color represents a different house, small and large all entangled. The red colored buildings are small, local chapels, the orange color represents the narrow lanes.

Lower-class Sumerians

Those who live in the poorer quarters of the city include craft workers, merchants, laborers, and peasants from among whom the army is also conscripted. In some merchants' quarters the houses are more substantial than those of the poor, and some men gain sufficient wealth to be included among the nobility and move to a better part of the city. Farmers also live inside the embankment, but during the planting and harvesting seasons, they go out to live in small houses on their farms—and hope there will not be any raids by the city's enemies.

Sleeping and eating

There is little furniture beyond chests, low tables, and stools, and at night people generally sleep on mats. Even in homes with more than one room, the family usually climbs onto the flat roof through the skylight for sleeping, because it's much cooler than inside—and it hardly ever rains.

Domestic utensils are mostly made of wood, bone, or sharpened flint because metal implements and vessels are too expensive for the poor. They do, however, have plenty of crockery because clay is plentiful and pots are cheap to barter for.

In crowded Ur, centuries of human waste and garbage thrown out on the alleyways has raised their height well above the original building level. The inhabitants have to cut steps into the side of the street to gain access to their homes.

An Aristocrat's House

The Sumerian aristocracy lives in exclusive precincts close to the religious complex and the royal palace. They include the priestly class, the king's ministers, senior bureaucrats, and very wealthy merchants.

For the aristocracy, life is luxurious. Slaves perform most of the menial tasks for a wealthy family, but their management is the responsibility of the women of the household. Women of the upper classes enjoy considerable freedom (*see page 34*).

They live in two-story brick-built houses with several rooms. To keep the rooms cool, the internal walls are whitewashed, and there are no windows. The rooms open onto a spacious courtyard, often planted with exotic flowers and fruits, which lets in plenty of light. There are separate bathrooms with their own plumbing, where slaves pour warm water over the bather and anoint, or rub their body, with precious oils.

1. The master of the house greets a caller in the reception room.

2. The household chapel, with a shrine standing next to the wall.

3. Steps lead down from the chapel to a large storage cellar.

4. One of the home's four bedrooms (the fourth is directly above); unlike poorer people, the rich sleep on beds.

5. In the long, narrow kitchen two slave girls are cooking a meal, using locally produced pottery bowls.

6. The tiled courtyard is open to the sky above. In its center there is a small drain, which serves two functions: drainage of the rare rainfall and for the ritual washing of a guest's feet.

7. One of several oil jars spread around the house. These contain different types of oil for cooking, lighting, and anointing the body.

8. General storage area.

9. Relaxation and dining room.

10. A wooden staircase gives access to the upper floor and a balcony overlooking the courtyard.

11. The mistress of the house gets dressed, ready to go downstairs and help her husband entertain their guests.

12. A slave tidies up a bedroom.

13. A second staircase leads up to the flat roof. Here the family often sleeps out on mats during the hottest weather.

14. A slave girl carries towels to the bathroom at the rear of the house beyond the stairs. The bathroom (**below**) houses a stone seat above drainage holes. A servant pours water from jugs over the bather. The water drains out into the yard.

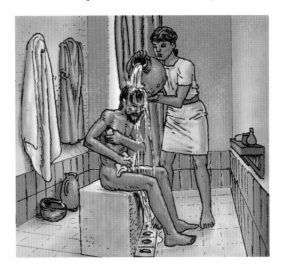

Sumerian Family Life—the Family Structure

The daily life of Sumerians is well documented, thanks to the invention of writing. The many relief carvings and statuettes put some color to the texts and help bring this vibrant culture to life.

In the homes of the poor and rich alike, the husband and father is the master of the household. He has the right to divorce a barren wife and to take concubines. He is even allowed, under certain circumstances, to sell his wife and children into slavery. Such a situation could arise from getting into debt to a man wealthier than himself, who would then take the debtor's family as slaves into his own household. In some cases, this fate may actually improve their lives.

Despite the husband's position, a woman of the upper class has considerable freedom. She has the right to own property and have an income separate from that of her husband. She is also allowed to offer evidence in a lawcourt case. But men make the major family decisions, such as arranging marriages for sons and daughters.

For the aristocrat, daily life is a round of organizing and planning his business ventures, tending to religious rites, and entertaining guests and visitors from other cities. At times of crisis, he is expected to serve as a military official and provide the city-state with produce and manpower from his farming estates.

Having received the bride price and consented to his daughter's marriage, the father adds his seal to the contract, while the bride's mother watches the happy couple.

Buying a slave

Slaves are prisoners of war or people hopelessly in debt in their community. In Mesopotamia, those most sought after for servitude are the men and women from the mountains to the north and northeast, the regions of Urartu and Lullu.

It is usually the task of wives to go to the market to purchase household slaves. The cost of a slave differs from city to city and from time to time, but averages between 30 and 40 *shekels* of silver, which is as much as the cost of three or four oxen. The best slave market in Sumer is at Eshnunna, between the important cities in the south and the hill country of Lullu.

A school for future officials

Boys of wealthy families attend school, while girls are educated at home. The school is located next to the royal palace, and is a part of the complex because the main object of education is to provide the king with more government officials. During the morning lessons, the boys practice their writing exercises. This involves copying words on a damp clay tablet from a list the teacher has prepared. As they do so, they must learn the meanings of the signs they are making.

Slovenly work earns a light blow with a wooden rod from the teacher across the pupil's shoulders. This is a common occurrence because pressing the reed stylus into the damp clay to make the wedge-shaped marks is tiring work—and mistakes are frequent.

The schoolboys are allowed a short break for lunch, probably of bread and figs that they have brought with them from home. Then it is time for the afternoon session of oral tests in language and arithmetic.

In the Sumerian world there is no safety net for failures, so—despite being very typical boys when it comes to school lessons—they take their work seriously. To be admitted into the palace bureaucracy when they are older will be the best possible start to their adult lives.

Death and burial

And when life comes to an end, Sumerians take the burial of the dead as seriously as any culture, though there are no cemeteries except for the king and his most important nobles. In Sumer the body is most often buried within the house in the family tomb (*see the illustration on page 32*). It may be laid to rest curled up and placed in a large jar, or extended in a casket, stone sarcophagus, or ordinary cloth wrapping.

The lavishness of the burial depends greatly on the economic status of the deceased, but Sumerians are usually buried surrounded by those possessions they most treasured in life. Some of the wealthiest men even have such grave goods specially made for their funeral, ensuring that everything they will need in the afterlife goes into their coffin with them.

Some pupils in a class of many at work on their lessons.

This is the sounding board of the magnificent lyre found in the queen's tomb. It is over 4500 years old.
The shell-decorated panels show four mythical scenes that were popular with the Sumerians of the period.

The Royal Tombs of Ur

These 16 tombs are the most celebrated yet uncovered. Located close to the palace, they date to about 2600 BCE. Grave robbers had stolen many of the grave goods, but the untouched tomb of Queen Pu-Abi revealed some beautiful objects. These included gold ribbon headdresses, gold vessels, bead pendants, lapis lazuli necklaces, a wooden lyre (*left*), a richly decorated royal sled, and precious jewels. There were also many bodies of sacrificed servants and slaves to accompany the queen on her journey and to serve her in the afterlife.

Queen Pu-Abi's body was covered with beads of precious metal, her fingers with rings, and the head adorned by a floral crown of metal and golden leaves (*above*).

Sumerian Family Life—Clothing and Adornment

The Sumerians use the natural resources available to them to make their clothing. The two main sources are sheep's wool and flax. Flax is a plant with blue flowers that grows well in a variety of conditions. Its tough stalk yields strong fibers, which can be processed and woven into cloth. Careful selection results in both coarse and fine fibers—better quality cloth is made from only the finest flax.

Men and women's clothing

In the early days, Sumerian men went barechested and barefooted through town, wearing only the traditional ringed kilt made from sheep's wool. Now they wear a long one-piece garment from shoulder to calf made from finely spun wool in the cooler season or at night, or from fine flax in the hotter periods.

Sometimes it has a decorative fringed shawl and a long fringed hem. On formal occasions priests still wear the traditional woolen kilt, and their long, trimmed beards usually distinguish them from lay nobles, those who serve the temple but aren't priests.

Women wear a full-length draped garment, which is typically worn with the right shoulder and arm free, or a fitted shoulder-to-ankle dress. Hair is worn in a wide variety of styles, in braids or coiled around the head, free-flowing with a decorative headband, or topped by a short, helmet-like hat. The hair is almost always perfumed.

This man's elegant clothing, with its long decorative fringe, indicates his status as a member of the wealthy administrative or land-owning class.

Figurines of men in prayerful attitudes, known as *orants*, are common in Sumer. The man on the right wears a long beard, indicating his position as a priest; both have typically heavily made-up eyes. The layering of their traditional woolen kilts is an effect derived from the pieced animal skins of the earliest days.

Jewelry and adornment

The Sumerian smiths can make fabulously elegant jewelry for adornment, and both men and women wear some, especially during religious festivals. Gold, silver and semi-precious stones are used to create necklaces, earrings, tiaras, finger rings, and bracelets. Beads of bright azure-blue lapis lazuli contrasting with the red carnelian are favorites.

Sumerian jewelers have discovered glass, made from heating soda with sand and limestone, and use it as a spectacular addition to gemstone jewelry. By adding different minerals to the glass, a rainbow of bright colors is achieved.

Women wear a full-length draped garment, which is typically worn with the right shoulder and arm free.

Sumerian women smooth their skin with a pumice stone and then contrast the eye make-up by painting their faces with white lead. This gives the face a mask-like appearance, and makes a base for the bright-red henna added to cheeks and lips. Henna is also painted on finger- and toenails, and sometimes on the palms of their hands.

Sumerians like to take regular baths in perfumed water, every day if possible, though the poor must make do with the nearby river or canal. After bathing, it's customary for a slave to rub his master's body with a perfumed oil (anointing), which serves a dual purpose—to make him smell pleasant in the company of others, but more importantly to repel the numerous insects flying and crawling around.

Men and women have many toilet articles, such as gold cosmetic cases, metal toothpicks, manicure kits, and eyebrow tweezers. The cosmetic cases, sometimes of shell as well as gold, contain the cakes of face paint in such colors as charcoal, brown, and blue for eye makeup.

A polished-bronze hand mirror is an essential aid when applying make-up. Jewelry, such as the headdress and earrings seen at lower left, add to a woman's natural beauty.

Black eyes and cosmetics

Men and women alike share a passion for cosmetics, and the height of beauty is considered to be heavily made-up eyes, faces, and hands—with an emphasis on the eyes. A bluish-black antimony—a brittle, crystalline metal compound—is used to line and highlight the eyes, and to blacken the eyebrows and eyelashes.

Sumerian Family Life—Daily Food

Early Mesopotamians ate anything they could catch in order to survive, and ate whenever they were hungry. But by this period food in Sumer is eaten as much for enjoyment as for nourishment. Evening meals—normally taken by most people before sunset, to make the most of the dwindling daylight—have become a form of entertainment for all except the poorest peasants.

Breakfast and lunch

With the huge grain harvests, the Sumerians' staple diet is of unleavened bread—a loaf similar to modern pita bread, baked without any rising agent such as yeast. Wheat and barley are partly ground to make a kind of porridge, which might be sweetened with dates or honey.

These ingredients make up the lesser meals of the day, breakfast and lunch, though lunch may be accompanied by dried or fresh fish and a variety of vegetables (see the list).

Varied fare

Common food for the ordinary Sumerian's evening meal consists of fish mixed with cucumber, onions, apples, spices, cheese, and eggs. The diet of wealthier people is much more varied. The livestock provide beef and mutton, while fish and wild fowl from the

Above: Cooled by an evening breeze, a prosperous family enjoys its rooftop meal. A lyre player and singer provide the entertainment.

The Sumerian diet

This list includes most of the foodstuffs eaten in Lower Mesopotamia. The better off you are, the more varied the daily diet.

beef	eggs	turnips
mutton	chickpeas	lettuce
pork	mustard	watercress
goat	onions	dates, fresh/dried
wild boar	garlic	honey
wild gazelle	leeks	cattle/goat's milk
wild fowl	beans	cattle/goat's cheese
deer/venison	lentils	barley cakes
fish	cucumber	wheat breads

Singers and musicians are revered in lower Mesopotamia through reliefs and statuettes. Many have enjoyed the singing voice of Ur-Nina (**right**) accompanied by the harpist from Isin-Larsa (**below**). Both date from about 2000 BCE.

The "Game of Ur," for two players, is a popular after-dinner entertainment for a quiet family evening.

river are popular, especially ducks. Hunters provide wild boar and venison. Fish is so plentiful that the city has many fish sellers and even restaurants where people can buy ready-cooked meals.

From the cattle, goats, and sheep comes milk, butter, and cheese, while the numerous palms provide dates. These are eaten fresh from the tree, dried, or pressed into a syrup.

The importance of honey

Honey is one of the most important ingredients for Sumerians—apart from the fig syrup, it is the only sweetener to add to food. In fact, honey is held in such esteem that it is used in religious ceremonies. It is poured over shrine thresholds and stones as a commemorative offering, and door bolts of sacred buildings are anointed with a mixture of honey and wine.

Honey has another important use—in making beer. This is the great Sumerian drink. There are 19 different kinds of beer, depending on the type of grain used in fermenting, the aromatic plants used for flavoring, and the variety of honey and malt added. Wine made from dates is also available, but not much is made, so it is expensive and restricted to the wealthy.

Poorer people only have water taken from the rivers to drink. This is kept in a long-spouted kettle that helps to filter out the muddy sediment.

After-meal entertainment

The Sumerians are a hospitable people who enjoy dining with friends or entertaining in their own homes. It is customary after a meal to relax while musicians, singers, and dancers perform for the guests. The city has many groups of entertainers for hire, but some of the richest families employ their own musicians and singers. Poets declaim the heroic deeds of mythical heroes and past kings, while music is played on the harp, lyre, and drum. And if the guests have any energy left after the meal, they can enjoy a board game.

The Government of Sumer, c.2300 BCE

As wars become more common between the city-states, *lugals* keep power for longer periods and eventually for life. From about 2900 *lugals* have become kings. They stand now at the head of a large administration.

The first kings had religious as well as administrative roles—they were priest-kings. But in the later Sumerian Period there is more separation between the king's role and that of the temple authorities.

The king is a representative of the gods, and may even claim to be a god himself. Although his position is a very powerful one, he is nevertheless dependent on the support of the priests who conduct the sacred ceremonies and act as judges in any legal disputes. This is derived from the story contained in the *Creation Epic*, in which even the gods must give their joint consent to the action of any other deity (*see pages 60–61*).

Tension between palace and temple

This priestly acceptance of his right to rule often creates tension between the palace and the temple. It sets the luxurious residence of the king, with its many annexes, administrative staff, and landed property, against the ritual and economic functions of the temple priests and stewards.

The king often appoints members of the royal household to important temple positions, and palace lands are sometimes assigned to priests, further blurring the division between palace and temple.

The temple administrators own as much as one-third of the city's land. They rent this out to local farmers in return for a share of the harvest. Temple lands and property really belong to the city's guardian god, and—in theory—the temple officials administer it on the deity's behalf.

The king's administration

The priest-king rules the city-state through many bureaucrats, a lot of them priests. They carefully survey the land, assign fields, and distribute crops after the harvest. These functions are important because the majority of people are city dwellers who no longer raise livestock or grow their own food.

This means that the relatively few farmers who grow the food to feed those who do

The Sumerian King List is far from complete. It does not, for instance, mention the city of Lagash, where Ur-Ningirsu (**left**) ruled 2122–2118 BCE in the recovery period after the Gutian kings (*see page 49*). One of the kings mentioned is Iku-Shamagan (**below**), who ruled in the city of Mari, c.3000 BCE.

The Sumerian King List

The Sumerians completed several lists of all their kings. These detail length of the kings' reigns and the cities they ruled. The most complete list was found at Nippur and dates from c.2125 BCE. The King List is not archaeologically accurate because some kings have unbelievably long reigns. For instance, the first dynasty of Kish claims that 23 kings ruled for 24,510 years, 3 months and 3.5 days—well over a thousand years each!

The list is divided into the period before and after the Great Flood, and the periods of rule given in the latter half are much more believable. The value of the King List is the insight it gives us into which Sumerian city was dominant in each period, and how power shifted from one city-state to another, often to and fro.

not must be subject to efficient management and a distribution system.

There are many other important bureaucratic functions. These include assessing how much tax each citizen must pay and collecting the tax goods, organizing the city's municipal workers, maintaining the defensive embankment and gates, and running the army. The elite of Sumerian society usually undertake these tasks—men who through increasing their land holdings have gained great wealth and become nobles.

The importance of record

The next layer of the government is even larger—the department of scribes. All this complicated administration can only work if every order given and every transaction made is recorded so that it can be checked at a later date.

When an official has to deal with 30 or 40 farmers, it is too much to expect him to remember six months later how much grain a farmer agreed he could harvest. And so, with their *cuneiform* writing system, hundreds of scribes act as secretaries to the bureaucrats.

In the same capacity scribes work for the temple, and of course for the king as well. In his service, senior scribes can become almost as distinguished as the nobility.

Honoring the city's gods

Above all, the king and his administrators must make sure that the people properly honor the gods through making regular sacrificial offerings (a form of temple tax), and by arranging the important religious festivals of the year. Without continual divine blessing, the city's fortunes will surely turn sour and more devout neighbors might gain a dangerous advantage.

Sumer runs on information. Every year each farmer is visited by a tax inspector who records his crop yield.

Temple administrators have an army of scribes to keep track of all their lands and produce, as well as the taxes owed.

A Visit to the Temple

The temple is the heart of the early Sumerian city-state. By the Early Dynastic Period, the era between 5000 and 4300 years ago, the temple has grown to become almost a city within the city.

Although the Sumerians believe in a collection of many gods—called a pantheon—each city has its own guardian deity, or patron god. This figurehead is one of the major gods, and his or her colleagues each control the powerful natural forces that dictate the fates of other Sumerian cities in the southern Mesopotamian plain.

These gods prefer justice and mercy, but unfortunately long ago they also created misfortune and evil. The ordinary Sumerian can do little to avoid whatever fate may be in store, but honoring the city's patron deity is believed to help. Unlike the domestic gods—who are satisfied with a simple form of worship—the city god demands a continuous flow of taxes to pay for the adornment of his temple.

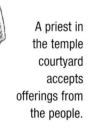

A priest in the temple courtyard accepts offerings from the people.

One temple on top of another

The Sumerians pay the tax by giving food, livestock animals, pottery utensils, and many other offerings to the temple priests. As the most senior of the priests, the king's most important task is to dedicate new temples as a sign of his devotion. This does not mean that he builds many new ones all around the city. Instead he lavishes his wealth by erecting a new one over the structure of an existing, older temple. And so, with each generation, the temple mound grows taller and larger in area.

It now resembles the sacred mountain of Ararat, where legend states that the first Sumerian king landed his boat after the Great Flood. Often—as illustrated here—one platform sits on top of a lower, wider one, and more will be added on top of that. This form of step-pyramid is called a ziggurat (from the Assyrian word *ziqquratu*, or "mountain top"). Later ziggurats will be far taller than this early example (*see pages 90–91*).

Many priests

The temple's inner precinct is called the *cella* and around its walls are many rooms to house the priests, priestesses, officials, musicians, and *hierodules*—slaves dedicated to the temple god. Under the king's divine guidance, these religious servants of the city god perform the daily public rituals and make food sacrifices from the offerings given by the people.

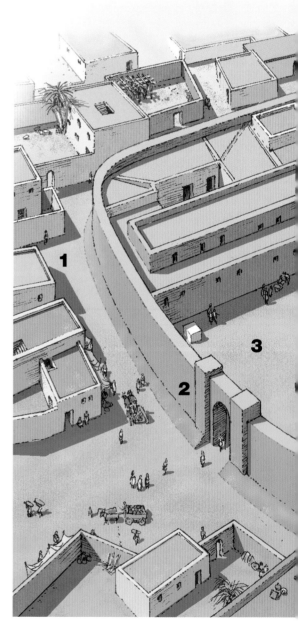

This reconstruction is based on the Oval Temple of a city called Khafaji, which is situated in the northern part of Babylonia.

1. The city dwellings cluster around the temple walls.

2. The main gate to the temple precincts.

3. The outer precinct includes storerooms and workshops. There are workshops for bakers, potters, weavers, and jewelers. It also acts as a gathering place for the city's inhabitants.

4. Sheep, goats, oxen, and donkeys are kept in special pens.

5. An arch leads to a stairway rising to the *cella*—the main temple precinct—on its higher platform. Here, the temple priests can be seen performing some of the daily rituals.

6. Residences of the priests and temple officials line the walls.

7. A second stairway climbs to a higher platform, on which stands the sanctuary.

8. The sanctuary houses an altar and an offering table. While senior priests and priestesses praise the god at the altar, a statue of the god stands behind the offering table, on which the food sacrifices are placed. The Sumerians believe that their gods reside in the temples from time to time, between their business in other parts of the country.

9. Since it rarely rains in Mesopotamia, families often sleep on the flat roofs.

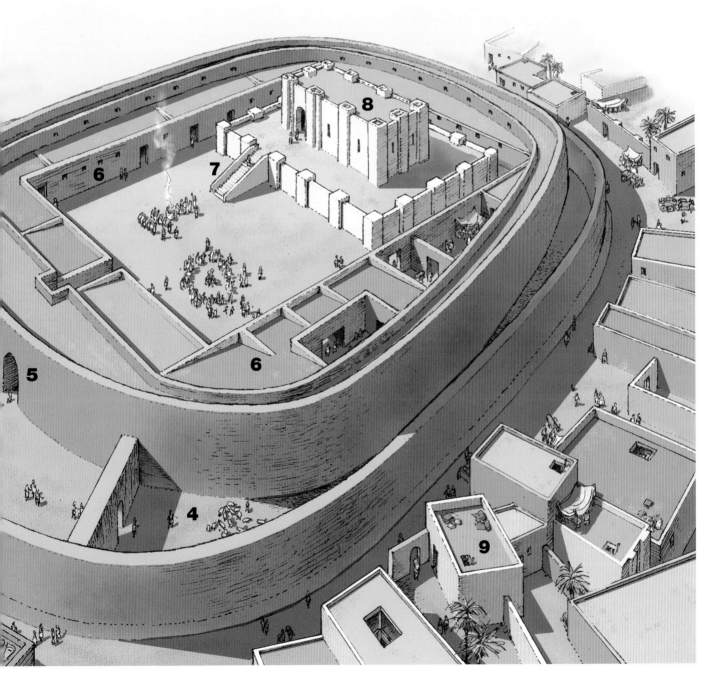

Worshipping the Gods

The Sumerians worship hundreds of gods who share the joys and failings of human emotions. They can be compassionate, but they can also vent their anger in the most terrible ways—in general the behavior of a god is never predictable.

The Sumerians have major deities who brought the world into being and control natural events. There are gods of the city-states and their rulers, deities of craftworkers, farmers, traders, and travelers, and minor gods of the home. The gods' lives were recorded and are kept up to date by the royal scribes, who have created a huge list of prayers, poems, and stories.

The Sumerian gods live in the same natural world as the humans. In the distant past the world was in a state of chaos until the great creation goddess Nammu gave it form and "gave birth to the numberless gods."

Creation of the world

Nammu created the sky and gave it to An, father of the gods, and she made the earth, which she gave to An's wife Ki. When they had a son, named Enlil, Nammu made him Lord Wind—he is the messenger between the sky and the earth. Enlil also owns the Tablet of Destiny, which controls the fate of the people. Enki (Lord Earth) controls fresh water and the flow of the Euphrates and Tigris on which survival depends. Ninhursag is the mother goddess and patron of fertility.

These major gods are assisted by a host of powerful deities. Nanna (the Moon) controls the months and seasons; he is the son of Enlil and Ninlil. Utu (the Sun) governs the days and dispenses justice. Ninurta protects farming but also controls storms. Inanna (Lady of Heaven) is the goddess of fertility, of life and death, and patron of granaries.

Making worshippers

When the gods had made harmony out of chaos, they came to realize that this happy state could only be maintained if there were beings to worship them. So they created people whose labors and offerings would be dedicated to maintaining the gods' positions. But the people were not always devout and so the gods sent a series of disasters, including the Great Flood, as punishment for human wrongdoing.

Over time, some humans became more powerful than others and were known as *lugals*, or great men. Some of these privileged men came to occupy high positions equal to their priest-rulers and eventually they became kings. Some of the nobles are considered to be gods. They are immortal and cannot die, so when their time on earth is finished they go to live with the other gods. For ordinary people death carries neither reward nor punishment—they simply turn to dust.

Divining the meaning of order

Much of Sumerian religion concentrates on divination—an attempt to predict what the gods' intentions might be. The regularity of the natural world—the seasons, and movements of the heavenly bodies—hold the key to the secret of order and so provide clues to what the gods are thinking.

The scribes, by recording the natural order, are therefore engaged in a sacred activity. Observation of the movements of the sun, moon, and stars leads to astrology and the acquisition of astronomical knowledge. This in turn requires complex mathematical calculations. More detail on these subjects may be found on pages 54–57.

Enlil, son of An and Ki, is the god of air and storms. He is supreme ruler of the Sumerian gods and guardian of the city of Nippur.

Above the earth, a great domed roof contains the sky, the stars, the moon, and the sun. Beneath the earth is the dark netherworld, abode of demons and the kingdom of the dead. Enlil and Enki created the cattle, sheep, the yoke, and the plow to provide food for the gods. But they were unable to make use of this bounty, so man was fashioned from clay that he might tend the sheep and cultivate the fields for the gods' benefit.

Utu (later Shamash), son of Nanna, is the sun god who lights the world with rays issuing from his shoulders. He is also the patron of justice, carved out with his saw.

Ninhursag, companion to Enlil and Enki, is Mother Earth, the source of all life and ensures the fertility of fields. She gave birth to all the plants.

Enki is the god of "sweet waters." He gives kings their wisdom to rule and is patron of crafts, learning, and magic.

Ereshkigal, sister of Inanna, is the goddess of darkness and death.

Ninurta, son of Enlil and his wife Gula, is the god of thunderstorms and the plow. As the "great hunter," he's also associated with Nimrud (of Nineveh) and the Babylonian god Marduk. To the later Assyrians, he is the god of war.

Inanna, daughter of Nanna, is the goddess of love and war (later renamed Ishtar). Inanna is present whenever life is conceived through love or ended in battle.

Nanna (*seen on the left from a carved relief*) son of Enlil, is the moon god, later renamed Sin. He decides the fate of the dead.

The ziggurat of Ur (**below**) measures about 150 by 200 ft and is 80 ft high. Its terraces are planted with trees so that it symbolizes the sacred mountain of Ararat. At the New Year ceremony, priests and *hierodules* bear the statue of Nanna the moon god, the city's patron deity, to his home on top of the ziggurat, as the cheering people honor his passage.

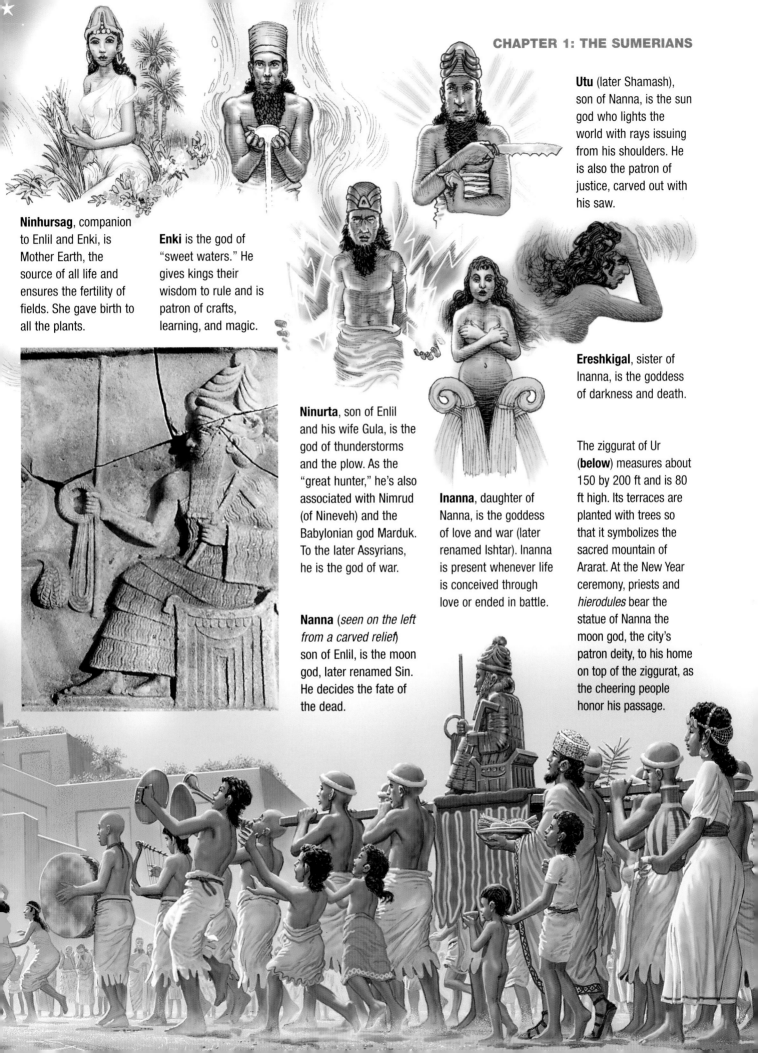

War Gets Organized

The Sumerian King List indicates how power constantly shifts between the many city-states as the warring dynasties struggle to become the dominant rulers of all Sumer.

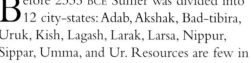

Before 2335 BCE Sumer was divided into 12 city-states: Adab, Akshak, Bad-tibira, Uruk, Kish, Lagash, Larak, Larsa, Nippur, Sippar, Umma, and Ur. Resources are few in these desert regions and that leads to intense competition for land and water. There are disputes over borders and rights of way that lead to constant warfare and power shifts in favor of the victorious king.

But because the Sumerians speak the same language regardless of which city they live in, and they worship the same gods, the power shifts have little impact on the ordinary people. A skilled army is nevertheless essential.

The Sumerian soldier

The Sumerian armies are better equipped and trained than those of surrounding tribes. The infantryman fights in a close order *phalanx* that takes a lot of training and organization. He is also better equipped than any foreign enemies.

A conical copper helmet with fixed cheek-pieces protects his head, and he wears a heavy woolen kilt sewn to a girdle fastened around the waist. He also has a long cloak of either animal skins or a heavy flaxen material, with copper, stone, or wood discs sewn on for added protection.

The weapons of bronze are stronger than those of any external foes. The soldier carries a spear, an ax, and a curved short sword. There are two types of spear. One is a long thin pike with a bronze head as much as two feet in length. The other is a broad, bronze leaf-shaped head of 12 to 20 inches long, sharpened along both edges so it can be used both for thrusting and slashing.

Two Sumerian heavy infantrymen survey the enemy. Both wear sheepskin kilts, and the warrior above is further protected by a thick metal-studded cloak. Helmets and weapons are of bronze.

The power of the chariot

Sumerians also use chariots, based on the four-wheeled farm cart, but with additional leather armor to protect the two-man crew of driver and warrior. The chariot body is square in shape with a step in the rear. At the front there are two round-topped shields and the reins pass between them. The chariots, which are pulled by four onagers, or wild asses, can manage a top speed of about 15 mph on level ground, but they are slow and clumsy in the turn. Chariots are best used for crashing through the enemy infantry line. The warrior uses several short spears, some modified for use with a throwing thong to gain distance, others for use in close combat.

Continual war weakens Sumer

While the Sumerians make war on external enemies, they are invariably the victors, but when they fight each other, it is hard to maintain the advantage for very long, and so first one and then another kingdom takes control of Sumer.

As early as 2600 BCE Gilgamesh of Uruk defeated the kings of Kish during an intense period of rivalry between Uruk, Kish, and Ur, and established sovereignty over these important city-states. Mesannepadda of Ur (c.2560–2525 BCE) defeated Agga of Kish and claimed all of

Sumer as his own. But by 2500 BCE the balance of power had shifted back to Kish.

Eannatum (2454–25), grandson of Ur-Nina of Lagash, defeated Umma and then conquered Ur, Uruk, and Kish, only to be overthrown soon after by Umma's forces. Fortunes were reversed again when Eannatum's nephew Entemena (2404–2375) defeated Umma.

Lagash lost its dominant position in 2350 when it was in turn conquered by Lugalzagesi of Uruk (2360–35), who was originally from Umma.

This continual fighting between the Sumerian city-states eventually weakened them to the point where they became vulnerable to enemies from beyond their borders. In 2340–2316 BCE Sumer, which had been united under Lugalzagesi, fell to the armies of King Sargon.

Sargon was not a member of one of the Sumerian dynastic families but came from a northern Semitic tribe. He was of humble origins, but had achieved a position of authority in the royal court at Kish, and by 2335 BCE he had made his own capital at Agade, or Akkad, after which his empire is known as Akkadian.

The two photographs on these pages show a Sumerian phalanx of infantrymen (**left**), a detail from the "Stela of the Vultures," which commemorates King Eannatum's victory over Umma, and a mosaic of a war chariot (**above**) carrying two warriors, trampling an enemy soldier to death, as recreated in the battle scene above.

Akkad Conquers Sumer

Having made Agade his capital, Sargon does not intervene to prevent Lugalzagesi's scheme to dominate Sumer. However, once Lugalzagesi has accomplished this, Sargon sends his Akkadian forces south to conquer unified Sumer.

Just five Akkadian kings ruled for a total of 150 years, yet their ideas have profoundly changed the language, art, religion, and culture of Mesopotamia. Their reformation of military tactics and law will persist for a further 2000 years, through the Babylonian and Assyrian periods, until the incursions of the Achaemenids from Persia in 539 BCE.

The Akkadian rulers

Though shrouded in mystery and legend, Sargon's prowess as a military leader and politician is denied by no one. His defeat of Lugalzagesi ends the independence of Sumer's city-states and brings in a new age of empire. Sargon was succeeded by two sons, Rimush and Manishtushu. Manishtushu was succeeded by his son Naram-Sin, who was followed in turn by his own son, Shar-kali-sharra, the last of the Akkadian kings.

Sargon justifies Akkadian rule by claiming that he has divine sanction and is descended from the goddess Ishtar, who is also the Sumerians' goddess Inanna (*see page 45*). He sets out to impress his new subjects through the arts, with the introduction of life-size heroic sculptures of himself and carved monumental victory columns, called *stelae* (*stela* in the singular).

Rebellious Sumer

As part of the process of unification, the Akkadians standardize weights and measures and insist on the use of the Semitic (Old Akkadian) language in all official documents. The establishment of a political capital at Agade and a religious capital at the holy city of Nippur further undermines the independence of the former city-states. But the Sumerians do not readily accept Akkadian rule. During Sargon's reign there are a number of local protests. These are quickly subdued, but on Sargon's death several of the cities, led by Ur and Lagash, stage an open rebellion that his son, Rimush, has great difficulty in subduing.

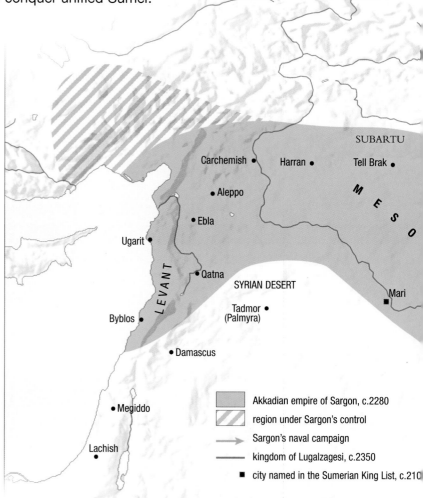

Akkadian empire of Sargon, c.2280

region under Sargon's control

Sargon's naval campaign

kingdom of Lugalzagesi, c.2350

■ city named in the Sumerian King List, c.210

Attacks by Nomads

King Naram-Sin (2254–17) engages in a series of extensive military campaigns in an attempt to consolidate Akkadian rule. He names himself King of the Four Regions—that is, king of the known civilized world—and calls himself God of Akkad. But despite being a god he is unable to rely on the loyalty of Lower Mesopotamia or, despite victories, eventually keep out such semi-nomadic tribes as the Elamites and Guti.

On his death in 2217, Naram-Sin's son Shar-kali-sharra proves to be a weaker leader. Under increasing pressure from the Elamites and Guti, he is forced to give up territory in the south and withdraw northward to the region around Agade.

A Babylonian cylinder seal of Ur-Nammu, depicts a goddess leading a worshipper before the deified king. Ur-Nammu was the first to set out a system of laws and penalties (*see page 52*).

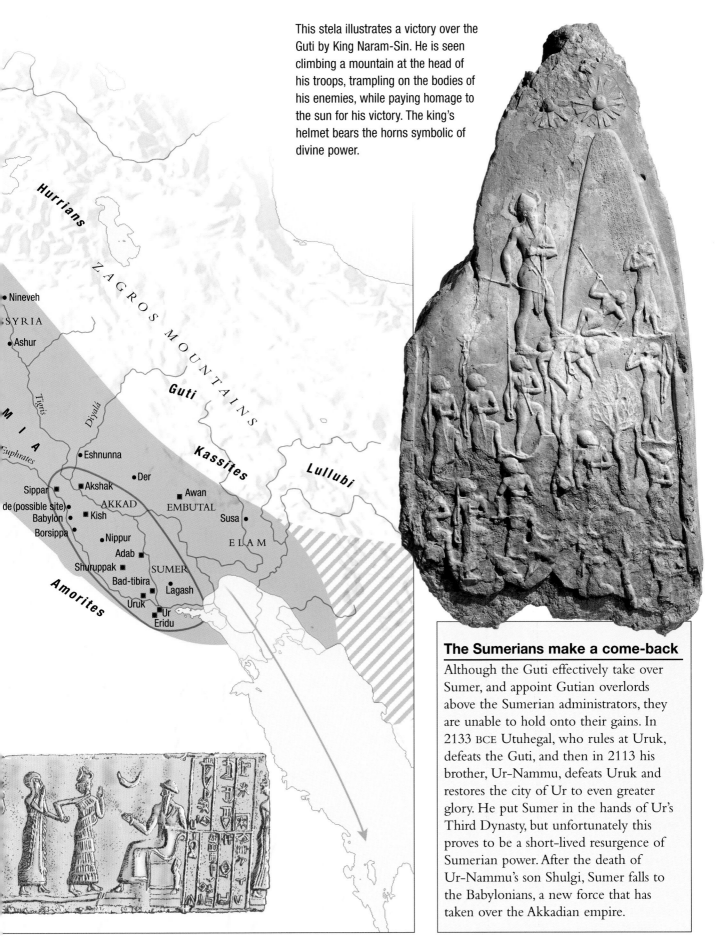

This stela illustrates a victory over the Guti by King Naram-Sin. He is seen climbing a mountain at the head of his troops, trampling on the bodies of his enemies, while paying homage to the sun for his victory. The king's helmet bears the horns symbolic of divine power.

The Sumerians make a come-back

Although the Guti effectively take over Sumer, and appoint Gutian overlords above the Sumerian administrators, they are unable to hold onto their gains. In 2133 BCE Utuhegal, who rules at Uruk, defeats the Guti, and then in 2113 his brother, Ur-Nammu, defeats Uruk and restores the city of Ur to even greater glory. He put Sumer in the hands of Ur's Third Dynasty, but unfortunately this proves to be a short-lived resurgence of Sumerian power. After the death of Ur-Nammu's son Shulgi, Sumer falls to the Babylonians, a new force that has taken over the Akkadian empire.

CHAPTER 2
Creating Order

The Legacy of Hammurabi

The last of the old Sumerian dynasties collapses in about 2000 BCE, after which Mesopotamia suffers a century of anarchy. But the great age of Sumerian culture is yet to come, and the first empire of Babylon ensures its triumph.

As the Third Dynasty of Ur falls apart, the power of Babylon rises. Before 2254 BCE Babylon has not even been mentioned in the Sumerian texts, so unimportant has this Amorite village been. But by 1900 BCE it has grown, thanks to a shift in the course of the Euphrates, which places it at the north end of the river's main stream and gives it a greater hold over trade. Under Hammurabi (c.1792–50 BCE), the dynasty's sixth king, Babylon grows to become one of the greatest empires of ancient times.

A new form of government

Hammurabi claims divine descent from Babylon's principal god, Marduk, a son of the Sumerian god Enlil. Through a combination of force and diplomacy, he welds together all of Mesopotamia, from the Persian Gulf to Nineveh. In so doing, the Babylonians absorb much of Sumerian culture, scientific knowledge, and religious beliefs. And so Babylonian culture is a combination of the earlier Akkadian and Sumerian beliefs and systems, but Hammurabi creates a completely centralized government in the capital, and his is now the only authority in the land.

After securing the immediate region of Lower Mesopotamia, he expands his empire. Over eight years, armies from Babylon defeat the cities of Larsa in the south, then Nineveh and Mari to the north, Eshnunna to the east, and the lands of the Guti as well.

Sumerian skills incorporated

With these victories, Babylonian control of trade throughout Mesopotamia is secured (*see "Hammurabi centralizes trade"*). Increases in trade result in the rapid development of early Sumerian mathematics, which soon becomes an area of scientific as well as economic activity. Other members of the literate

Statuette of King Hammurabi kneeling in prayer.

The empire of Hammurabi

Third Dynasty of Ur, 2112–04 BCE
Ammorite kingdom, c.1813–1780 BCE
Empire of Hammurabi, c.1750 BCE

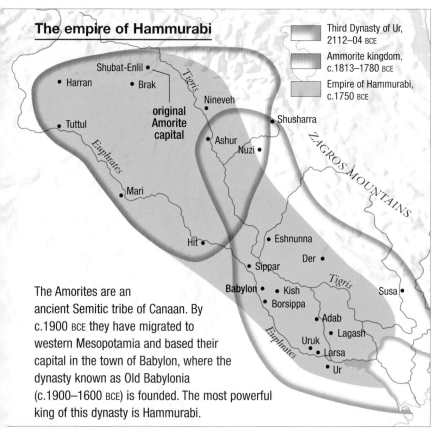

- Harran
- Shubat-Enlil
- Brak
- Tuttul
- Nineveh
original Amorite capital
- Ashur
- Shusharra
- Nuzi
- Mari
- Hit
- Eshnunna
- Der
- Sippar
- Babylon
- Kish
- Susa
- Borsippa
- Adab
- Lagash
- Uruk
- Larsa
- Ur

Tigris
Euphrates
ZAGROS MOUNTAINS
Tigris
Euphrates

The Amorites are an ancient Semitic tribe of Canaan. By c.1900 BCE they have migrated to western Mesopotamia and based their capital in the town of Babylon, where the dynasty known as Old Babylonia (c.1900–1600 BCE) is founded. The most powerful king of this dynasty is Hammurabi.

elite—scribes, doctors, and teachers of language and literature—follow suit to become distinct professional groups with high social standing, separate from the priesthood. Perhaps Hammurabi's greatest accomplishment is to take the laws of Ur-Nammu as a basis for a complete overhaul of the law (*see the following pages*).

In his throne room, **right,** Hammurabi holds an audience with visiting officials from Lower Mesopotamia.

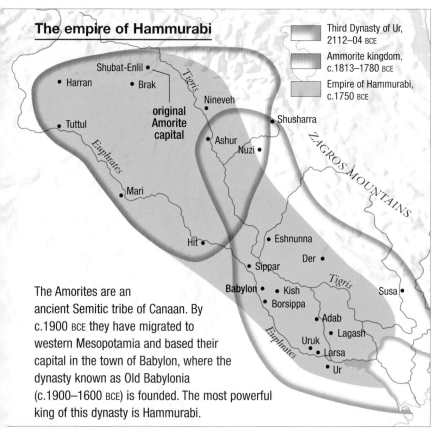

Horses are a wonder to the Sumerians, astonished at their speed and elegance.

Hammurabi centralizes trade

Mesopotamian trade has expanded greatly under the Babylonians. This is principally in foodstuffs, mostly dates and grain, but also includes silver, gold, lapis lazuli and carnelian gems, exotic woods and aromatic oils, perfume, tin, copper, wool, textiles, fish, and slaves. Horses—which first start to arrive from the Asian steppes in about 2000 BCE—are also an important commodity.

Merchants travel between cities in caravans—often with armed guards to protect them from bandits—and local agents act as brokers. Goods are traded in their silver value and trade is so profitable that merchants can receive as much as 100 percent return on their investment.

Making New Laws

First Ur-Nammu and then, 300 years later, Hammurabi change the lives of ordinary people forever through their codes defining the laws of the land.

The *mashkim*, or court clerk, records the proceedings of a trial as the defendant attempts to clear his name before three judges.

The laws of the Sumerian King Ur-Nammu are the oldest known in the world. They outline a policy of tolerance and equality and make no distinctions for a person's wealth or status. They specify fines for breaking the law, rather than corporal punishment, even for crimes of assault.

The laws deal with everyday matters, such as the return of a slave to his master, and less common accusations of witchcraft. Ur-Nammu's concern for the welfare of ordinary citizens is plain when he states that the laws are intended to ensure that "the orphan does not fall a prey to the wealthy" and "the widow does not fall a prey to the powerful."

Hearing a court case

A court consists of three or four judges, drawn from the ranks of temple administrators, sea merchants, scribes, and city elders. Judges are assisted by the *mashkim*, a court clerk, who records every detail of the case.

When a victim lodges a complaint he must swear an oath that his complaint is just, and provide evidence and witnesses who can support the accusation. Witnesses give their statements under oath, which the *mashkim* records on a clay tablet. The verdict and the payment date of the penalty decided are also inscribed, and the tablet countersigned by the judges, the *mashkim*, witnesses, and prosecutors. A completed case record is called a *ditilla* and deposited in the court archive.

An eye for an eye…

The Code of Hammurabi is much harsher than Ur-Nammu's. Based on the principle of "an eye for an eye," it begins and ends with addresses to the gods, asking them to ensure that any punishment is fairly carried out. It contains 282 judgments on a variety of topics, in which punishment is made according to the nature of the original crime.

Where Ur-Nammu's laws are the same for everyone, Hammurabi's divide the population into three groups. The *amelu* are land-owners with full citizenship, who have certain rights and privileges but are subject to higher fines and heavier punishments for their crimes. The *muskinu* are people defined

This detail from the top of the Stela of Hammurabi shows the king receiving the Law from the sun god Shamash (the Sumerian god Utu, who is also the patron of Justice).

Justice for the helpless

Despite the code's harshness compared to Ur-Nammu's, Hammurabi's laws are fairly administered, and suspicion of a crime is not sufficient to result in conviction. The judges, witnesses, and other interested parties sign the decision, and an oath is taken to pledge that the verdict will be adhered to. Like Ur-Nammu, Hammurabi sets out his reasons for formulating them, so "that the strong may not oppress the weak [and] to see that justice is done for the orphan and widow."

"If a son strikes his father, they shall cut off his hand."

"If a nun who is not living in a convent opens a wine shop or enters a wine shop for a drink, she will be burned."

"If a house collapses through faulty building and causes the death of the owner of the house, the builder shall be put to death."

"If bad characters gather in the house of a wine seller and she does not arrest those characters and bring them to the palace, she will be put to death."

as not owning any land. Finally, the *ardu*, or slaves, are captives or free citizens who have been sold into slavery for being in debt. If an *ardu* wins compensation in a case, it is paid to his master.

Punishments to fit the crime

The code also deals with the sale, lease, loan, and barter of property. Marriage contracts give women considerable rights over dowries, ownership of property, and custody of children. If a wife is unable to bear children, the husband may take a second wife with his first wife's agreement, but she remains her husband's responsibility. Children must care for their elderly parents, although they can buy a slave to do the job for them.

Apart from fines, the most common punishments are exile, public whipping, and removal from office. Serious crimes are sometimes punishable by death, including adultery, burglary, illegal entry to the temple or palace treasuries, handling stolen goods, kidnapping, hiding fugitive slaves, or for causing death from the collapse of a carelessly built house.

"If a man is unable to pay his debts, he must sell his wife, son, or daughter, or bind them over to service of another for three years."

"If a judge makes an error in his judgment through his own fault, he must pay 12 times the fine he set."

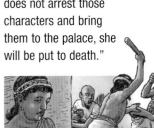

Set rates of pay for laborers

An ox-driver is paid 6 *gur* of corn per year. A field-hand may be hired for no less than from April to August at a daily rate of 6 *gerahs*, and from August until the end of the year at 5 *gerahs* per day (to take into account the shorter working day). The hire fees for an ox for threshing grain is 20 *ka* of corn per day, for an ass also 20 *ka,* and for a "young animal" 10 *ka* of corn. An ox, cart, and driver will be paid 180 *ka* of corn per day and the cart alone 40 *ka*.

Reaching for the Heavens

The Sumerians invented simple mathematics to help them accurately record quantities in transactions, but it is the Babylonians who raise arithmetic to the sophisticated level that make it the basis for future scientific discovery.

The Babylonian clay tablet on the opposite page is a student's calculation of a complex algebraic equation, dating from about 2000–1600 BCE. It indicates just how hard young scholars have to work.

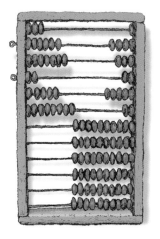

An ancient abacus.

This diagram shows how the Babylonians use what is called a "positional base-60 system." In some ways it is similar to the decimal, or base-10 system in use today. This is because the 59 numbers are built from a single symbol configured in nine different ways, and a "ten" symbol configured in five different ways.

The Sumerians at first used a single clay token to represent a single object, such as one sheep, or one measure of grain. As trade increased, the larger numbers that were recorded on clay tablets meant using tokens that had multiple values.

In this way the number 11 is shown by one token representing ten units and another representing a single unit following it. The "place values" of the counters is similar to the way a decimal point is used today.

How Babylonians count

To make calculation easier, the Babylonians use the abacus, invented by the Akkadians. With several layers, the abacus—seen on the left here—makes it possible to do much more extensive additions, subtractions, and even multiply or divide numbers.

The more sophisticated Babylonian system has a base number of 60—which survives today in the hour of 60 minutes, the minute

of 60 seconds, and a circle of 360 degrees (six times 60). The panel below shows how the place values work. The Babylonians have also refined Sumerian ideas of measures of length, area, capacity, and weight and given them standard values.

Theory in practice

Now Babylonian mathematicians can solve complicated problems, such as finding a market rate for goods of differing type, measuring lengths of canals, calculating weights of stones, areas of fields, or the number of bricks needed for a construction.

They can also calculate the number of workers and days necessary for building a canal, and the total wages needed for its workers. Some scholars have developed skills far beyond those needed for daily life, and these students are selected for special attention, some of them tutored to enter the privileged priesthood.

The Sumerian and Babylonian counting system

1		11		21		31		41		51	
2		12		22		32		42		52	
3		13		23		33		43		53	
4		14		24		34		44		54	
5		15		25		35		45		55	
6		16		26		36		46		56	
7		17		27		37		47		57	
8		18		28		38		48		58	
9		19		29		39		49		59	
10		20		30		40		50			

The ziggurat as practical mathematics

The ziggurat is the greatest surviving evidence of Babylonian mathematics. It would have been impossible to lay out and construct one without the tools of algebra and trigonometry. There have been many attempts to prove that the various dimensions in a Babylonian ziggurat are derived from what are sometimes called "sacred calculations."

This theory suggests that Babylonian astronomers are able to measure the distances between Earth and celestial bodies like the sun, moon, and the visible planets. Tables are then employed to calculate the proportions of a ziggurat so that its width, height, and number of platforms are in perfect harmony with the heavens.

The invention of equations

Babylonian mathematicians have also developed "tables," which speed up the process of complex calculations. They have tables for multiplication, square and cube roots, and reciprocals (used in division). By consulting a conversion table, the difference in value of goods traded from one place to another can be quickly determined, as well as the value of goods in the same weight of silver.

Although most of these tables indicate that Babylonian mathematicians think more in terms of abstract arithmetic—logarithms and algebraic equations—they know the concept of *pi* to work out the area of circles (1200 years before Pythagoras of Greece). And despite an emphasis on theoretical calculation, Babylonian engineers are very practical in applying geometry (earth measurements) to determine length, area, and volume when it comes to the construction of buildings and irrigation canals.

Reading the Heavens

With their advanced mathematics, the Babylonians are capable of more accurate astronomical predictions than the Sumerians had been. To the Mesopotamians, astronomy, astrology, and the calendar are intimately linked.

The Sumerian and Babylonian astronomers do not have telescopes, and so their observations are all made by the unaided eye. Their efforts, therefore, concentrate on those most visible of the heavenly bodies—the sun, the moon, the nearer planets (Mercury, Venus, Mars, Jupiter, Saturn), and the brightest stars.

Creating the calendar

The astronomers study the heavens to discover the seasonal patterns that are all important to farmers in order to establish an accurate calendar. This is done by recording and calculating the behavior of the sun and moon. The moon's 28-day cycles give a year of 12 lunar months of 29 or 30 days—with a few odd days left over.

To keep the lunar year in step with the solar year, the priests decree the addition of an intercalary, or extra, month to the calendar every three years or so, making a year of 13 months. The Sumerian year begins after the harvest, in September/October, but the Babylonians start the calendar year in spring.

Months and seasons

There are only two seasons. *Emesh*, the dry, growing season begins in February/March, in time to benefit from the annual flooding in April/May of the Tigris and Euphrates from snow melting in the Armenian Mountains. *Eten*, or winter, begins in September/October with the arrival of the rains, although these are usually limited to a few showers in Lower Mesopotamia.

Each month starts at the first sighting of the new moon. Because there is no universal naming system for the months between all the Mesopotamian cities, scribes give the months a number from the start of the New Year.

The Mesopotamian week

The moon goes through four phases in each month, and these "quarters" produce the concept of the seven-day week, although for the ordinary Mesopotamian the work cycles change only between holy days.

These are usually celebrated on the first, seventh and fifteenth of each month. Each city has its own additional feast days, which vary from place to place.

Right: Hammurabi's astronomer, identified by pendants representing Venus and the constellation Leo, informs the king that an intercalary month is due, and Hammurabi consequently instructs his senior minister to alter the date for collecting taxes.

Center: Astronomers and astrologers standing on top of a ziggurat note the moment of the new moon's rising.

Astrology and men's fate

The Babylonians divide the sky into zones for observation. The most important is the zone that lies along the celestial equator (ecliptic), the apparent path followed by the sun, moon, and planets across the sky. By continual recording of these movements, astronomers can now make predictions based on studying past records rather than by observation.

Examining the sky is the preserve of the astrologers who observe the movements of the planets and brightest stars to cast horoscopes that predict the future.

Isolated events, such as a planet's first and last appearances in the sky and the times at which that happens, can foretell human fate. We learn that *"When a halo surrounds the moon and Jupiter stands within it, the King of Akkad will be besieged,"* or *"When Mercury is visible with Mars at sunset there will be rains and floods. When Jupiter appears at the beginning of the year, in that year its crops will prosper."*

Almost all of these kinds of astrological prediction concern either the fates of the ruling elite or the well-being of the food supply, and consequently the state of the produce market.

Mesopotamian astronomers use the skies to help regulate the world's natural cycles, while astrologers interpret the heavenly movements as the designs of the gods who control all things.

Hours of the day

The day starts at sunset and is divided into six "watches." Each watch lasts about four hours.

Daytime Watches:

1st Watch	Morning	8:00 am–midday
2nd Watch	Midday	midday–4:00 pm
3rd Watch	Afternoon	4:00 pm–8:00 pm

Nighttime Watches:

1st Watch	Evening	8:00 pm–midnight
2nd Watch	Starlight	midnight–4:00 am
3rd Watch	Dawn	4:00 am–8:00 am

The length of a Sumerian hour varies according to the season because an hour is measured as being one-sixth of the available daylight; a summer hour is longer than a winter hour because the summer day is longer.

Medicine in Mesopotamia

The work of the Mesopotamian doctor involves prayer, magic, and a surprisingly successful mixture of herbal remedies. But for failure, the surgeon risks a severe penalty.

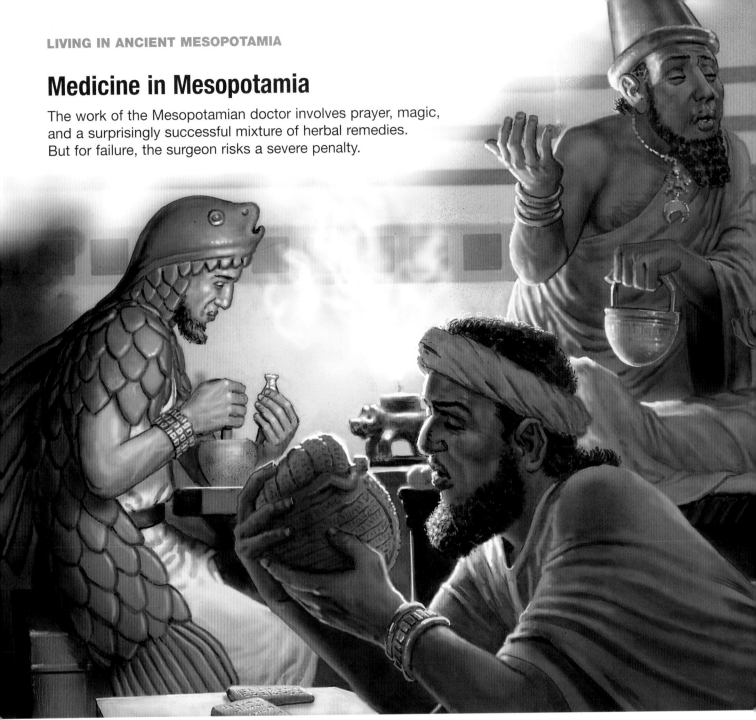

Disease in Mesopotamia is usually blamed on an evil spirit or the punishment of the victim by an angered god. It follows that the remedy for such an affliction is either to drive out the evil spirit or to make amends to the god in question. For this purpose the patient must call on an *ashipu*, or sorcerer.

Driving out evil spirits

The *ashipu*'s first task is to diagnose the ailment. In the case of internal diseases, this means finding out which god or demon is causing the illness. Having discovered the culprit, the *ashipu* next attempts to discover if the disease is the result of some error or

sin on the patient's part. Demons are hard to appease, but the patient can help his cure from a divine illness by praying to the god for forgiveness of his sin.

In the case of a demon, the *ashipu* might attempt to cure his patient by means of spells and magic potions designed to entice away or drive out the offending spirit.

Herbal remedies

As well as magical rites, practical remedies are also available. For this purpose the *ashipu* can refer the patient to an *asu*, or physician, a specialist in herbal remedies. However, the *asu* is less used to dealing with internal

The penalty for failure

Sometimes an *asu* is called on to perform surgery, for instance cutting into the patient's chest in order to drain pus from around the lungs. However, this carries a risk for both patient and doctor. According to the Code of Hammurabi, an *asu* is held responsible for any surgical errors caused by "the use of a knife."

If a surgeon saves the life of a person of high status, he receives a fee of 10 *shekels* (he only receives 2 *shekels* for a slave). If he should cause the death of a slave, the *asu* only has to pay the slave's master the price to replace him. But if a noble should die under the knife, the surgeon risks having his right hand cut off.

The *asu* often works together with an *ashipu*, especially if the patient is wealthy enough to afford both their fees. They might also work with an omen priest. This man divines the causes of disease by examining a clay model of a sheep's liver. The model is inscribed with diagnoses based on the livers of real sheep slaughtered in the past for the purpose of reading omens.

Belief is all

While many of the herbal remedies used in Mesopotamian medicine—plant extracts, resins, and spices—have antibiotic properties and some antiseptic value, others have no beneficial effect beyond masking the bad smell of an infected wound. But because the patients truly believe the doctors are capable of healing them, it gives them the will to overcome many illnesses.

diseases, since he usually treats maladies that can easily be seen, such as wounds.

In his medical armory the *asu* has dressings, plasters, and poultices to bind wounds and reduce infection. Many of these include the use of salt as an antiseptic and saltpeter (potassium nitrate) as an astringent, to harden the skin and reduce bleeding.

Washing the infected area is also important, and Mesopotamian doctors often wear a costume that makes them resemble a fish, one symbol of Enki, god of the "sweet waters." The techniques of the *asu* appear in the world's oldest known medical document (*see "Curing a wound"*).

An anxious father watches over his sick son, who holds out his hands in prayer, while an *ashipu*, with his right hand held wide in a similar gesture, attempts to expel the demons suspected of causing the illness. An *asu* in the corner prepares a herbal remedy, while an omen priest consults a model of a sheep's liver.

Curing a wound

One of the world's earliest prescriptions, for an infected limb, dates from 2100 BCE: "Pass through a sieve and then knead together turtle shells, salt, and mustard. Then wash the diseased part with good beer and hot water, and rub with the mixture. Then rub again with oil, and put on a poultice of pounded pine."

Mesopotamian Literature—Creation and Gilgamesh

Sumerian writing was first used for practical purposes, such as administrative records, but it soon flowers into the more exciting sphere of telling stories—the birth of literature.

In the Creation Myth, Marduk battled with Tiamat, destructive goddess of chaos.

No one knows who wrote the two great works of Mesopotamian literature, the *Eridu Genesis* (or *Creation Epic*) and the *Epic of Gilgamesh* because they moved from purely spoken legend to words on clay tablets over hundreds of years, and are known in various versions.

The promotion of Marduk

The *Creation Epic* is the mythic account of the world's origin and of the first king, who descended from Heaven to take up residence in the city of Eridu. The story mainly concerns the battle between the good gods against the powers of chaos, led by the destructive goddess Tiamat.

None of the gods had the courage to oppose her, but Enki designated young Marduk as the leader most likely to succeed. Marduk agreed, but only in return for being made the most senior of the gods. No act of such importance could be applied unless approved by the full assembly of the gods.

Shrewd Enki knew there would be objections from the older gods, so he called them all to a great banquet. By the time he got around to discussing his plan, his guests had all drunk so much wine that they agreed without argument.

Armed with his new authority, Marduk eventually defeated Tiamat and sliced her body in half. Her waters formed the clouds and her tears turned into the Tigris and the Euphrates rivers. In this story, the Sumerians learn that even the gods must consult one another before taking a decision, and all the kings who follow must also agree to rule, like the gods, by discussion and consent.

The search for eternal life

The world's oldest recorded story, the *Epic of Gilgamesh*, tells of the hero's quest to learn the secret of eternal life. The warlike Gilgamesh leads his companion Enkidu, Lord of the Wilderness, from the city of Uruk on a fantastic journey to the distant Land of the Forest of Cedars. After overcoming many dangers placed in their way, they reach the forest and defeat its guardian, a giant named Humbaba.

Returning to Uruk, they discover the city threatened by a divine bull, sent by Inanna, the goddess of fertility, who also holds the power of life and death. The heroes defeat the bull and prevent Uruk's destruction, but their success reminds the gods that the people they created should not become too powerful.

The gods decide that Enkidu must die, and his sudden death fills Gilgamesh with a fear of his own end. He is driven to despair—his only hope is to find the plant that can give him eternal life. This he learned from his ancestor Uta-napishtim, who claimed to be the sole survivor of the Great Flood.

Success and failure

Gilgamesh's search for the plant is successful, but he leaves it unguarded and a serpent carries it off. In desperation Gilgamesh turns to Enkidu's ghost for consolation. The ghost, however, tells him that the dead should not expect to be revered by the living and reminds him that humans "become dust" when they die. His great quest has been a failure, but the end of the story finds Gilgamesh at peace with himself and his surroundings.

The epic poem includes many aspects of daily life, but its most important message is that even the semi-divine king must die one day, and that royalty must be renewed from generation to generation.

Above: Gilgamesh and Enkidu face Inana's divine bull. They defeat it to save Uruk from destruction.
Left: In a Sumerian relief, Gilgamesh wrestles with lions. Gilgamesh is both a historical and a legendary figure. In his historical role he rules Uruk in about 2600 BCE. He is credited with establishing Uruk as a model city and for bringing civilization to the previously untamed world.

The Great Flood

In the Land Between the Rivers, floods are frequent events. Some are so powerful they can wipe out a city and its people. The flood of the Gilgamesh legend is the same as the one mentioned in the Bible, and Uta-napishtim is the equivalent of Noah and his Ark.

Exit From Ur—the Spread of Mesopotamian Culture

Now the Lord said to Abraham, "Go from your country and from your kindred and your father's house, to the land that I will show you." — *Genesis 12:1*

Below: Merchants carry weighing scales with them to ensure the fairness of transactions in foreign countries.

Facing below: Two merchants bargaining.

Thanks to the Bible, Abraham is the most famous inhabitant of Ur. The Old Testament tells the story of how Terah took his son Abraham and his grandson Lot, together with Abraham's wife Sarai, and left "Ur of the Chaldees" (*see "The lost Ur"*) to travel to Haran, almost 800 miles away.

At Haran Terah died, and Abraham became the leader of his clan. And here, God directed him to Canaan to found the nation of Jews. Famine later drove Abraham's family to Egypt, but on their return their flocks had prospered and they split up. Abraham made his home first in Hebron and then Bethel, while Lot eventually settled in the twin cities of Sodom and Gomorrah.

Abraham also visited Sodom and Gomorrah when God was poised to destroy the settlements because of the inhabitants' evil behavior. Abraham pleaded that the devout be spared. His nephew Lot and family were saved by angels while "fire and brimstone" rained down. Famously, Lot's wife could not contain her curiosity and turned to look back, against divine orders. She was turned into a pillar of salt.

Mesopotamians on the move

There are many theories about the story of Abraham, whether it represents the adventures of one person, or a combination of several people, and there is debate on how much is legend and how much is based on truth. It certainly represents how merchants spread Mesopotamian culture beyond the boundaries of Sumer and Babylon.

At the time in question—according to most scholars, some time between 1900 and 1750 BCE—Lower Mesopotamia was suffering the upheaval that followed the collapse of the Third Dynasty of Ur, and it is believable that many merchants decided to

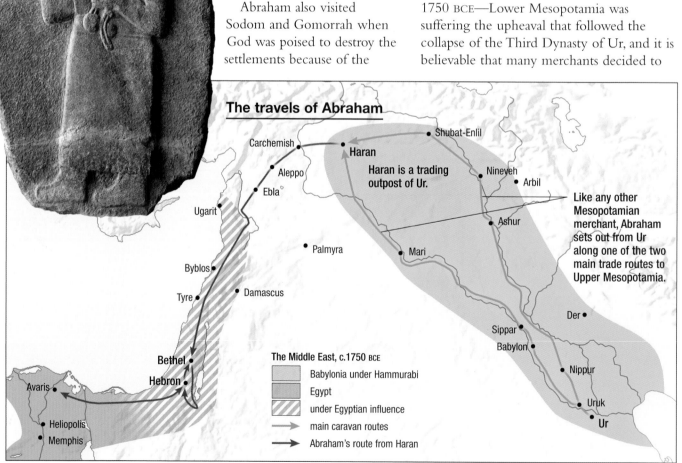

The travels of Abraham

Shubat-Enlil

Carchemish

Haran

Haran is a trading outpost of Ur.

Nineveh

Arbil

Aleppo

Ebla

Ugarit

Ashur

Like any other Mesopotamian merchant, Abraham sets out from Ur along one of the two main trade routes to Upper Mesopotamia.

Palmyra

Mari

Byblos

Tyre

Damascus

Der

Sippar

Babylon

Bethel

The Middle East, c.1750 BCE

Nippur

Hebron

Avaris

Babylonia under Hammurabi

Egypt

under Egyptian influence

main caravan routes

Abraham's route from Haran

Uruk

Ur

Heliopolis

Memphis

move to quieter Upper Mesopotamia. And while it was a long way, Mesopotamian trade caravans regularly made journeys of this length.

Handing over the alphabet

Abraham must have been only one of many Sumerians and Babylonians traveling to Upper Mesopotamia in search of trade. These merchants carried with them the arts of writing and mathematics, which spread between the cultures of the region and eventually to the Mediterranean coast.

By the 13th century BCE, the Syrian trading kingdom of Ugarit had developed the Sumerian *cuneiform* into a 30-character alphabet. In turn, this was later adapted by first the Phoenicians, then the Greeks and Romans into the one we know today.

Giving up the Sumerian gods

Of course, Abraham's biblical significance is in his being the founding father of Judaism, although his conversion to the worship of "the one and only god" Jehovah remains a mystery. We have only the Old Testament's version, and this assumes that the god he spoke to was God of the Bible.

Yet, as a Sumerian, Abraham may have worshipped the many Sumerian gods of his childhood, and Haran where he first settled was the center for worship of Sin (Nanna), the moon god.

Development of the alphabet from *cuneiform* to Latin

Ugarit		Phoenician		Greek		Latin
▶▶⊢	'a	ALEPH	⋉	ALPHA	A	A
	b	BETH	ℊ	BETA	B	B
	g	GIMEL	⅂	GAMMA	Γ	C
	d	DALETH	⊲	DELTA	Δ	D
	h	HE	⋀	EPSILON	E	E
	w	VAV	⅄			F
	ch					
		HETH	ꓧ	ETA	H	H
	th	TETH	⊕	THETA	Θ	
	y	YOD	⅄	IOTA	I	I
	k	KAPH	⅄	KAPPA	K	K
	ss					
	l	LAMED	⎣	LAMBDA	Λ	L
	m	MEM	⋔	MU	M	M
	td					
	n	NUN	⅂	NU	N	N
	s	SAMEK	≢	XI	Ξ	
	gh	AYIN	O	OMICRON	O	O
	p	PE	⅂	PI	Π	P
	ts	SADE	⋎			
	q	KOPH	℗			Q
	r	RESH	⅊	RHO	P	R
	sh	SHIN	W	SIGMA	Σ	S
	gh					
	t	TAW	⊤	TAU	T	T
				UPSILON	V	V
				PHI	Φ	
				CHI	X	X
				PSI	Ψ	
	z	ZAYIN	I	ZETA	Z	Z
				OMEGA	Ω	
	i,e					
	o,u					
	s2					

The lost Ur

The Bible refers to Abraham's birthplace as Ur of the Chaldees. When the books of the Old Testament were compiled, Ur had been abandoned. In order to give their readers an idea of where it lay they used the word Chaldees to indicate that it was in southern Babylonia, which at the time was also known as Chaldea.

CHAPTER 3
The Age of Super States

Indo-Europeans Occupy Mesopotamia

Upper Mesopotamia undergoes sweeping changes after 2000 BCE as a series of new peoples enter the region. Modern scholars know them as Indo-Europeans. Some settle, others move on, seeking new territories to conquer.

The Indo-Europeans originally came from the great plains, or steppes, that stretch from Mongolia, through southern Russia and into central Europe. One race, the Mycenaeans (named after the site where their culture was first discovered), settled in Greece in about 1900 BCE. Further east, Indo-Europeans known as Aryans settled in Persia and northwest India in about 1500 BCE. All these people spoke a related language and they had something else important in common—they were horsemen.

The Hurrians

Toward the end of the third millennium BCE, the Hurrians seem to have migrated from the region between the Black and Caspian Seas called Urartu (modern Armenia). They established kingdoms in Upper Mesopotamia and later united with the Mitanni. The Hurrians also moved to the southwest of the Fertile Crescent, eventually forming a ruling elite in many cities in Canaan. They may even have formed a part of the nation known as the Hyksos, who invaded Egypt in about 1640 BCE.

The Mitanni

The Mitanni were Indo-Europeans related to the Hurrians. They settled in Upper Mesopotamia in about 1500 BCE and united the Hurrian kingdoms into a single state under their rule. In 1450–1390 BCE they built up an empire that stretched from the Mediterranean to the Zagros Mountains. This brought them into conflict with the Egyptians, but the two nations made peace in about 1400 BCE. The Mitanni were fine horsemen and even wrote books on horse management. In about 1370 BCE the Hittites attacked the western part of the Mitanni kingdom, after which their state broke up.

The Hittites

Another Indo-European race, the Hittites settled in Anatolia (a part of modern Turkey) in about 2000 BCE. By about 1740 BCE the Hittites were united under one ruler, and occupied almost all of Asia Minor. At its height between 1600 and 1200 BCE, the Hittite empire extended from Mesopotamia to Syria and Palestine.

They conquered Babylon in about 1595 BCE, overthrowing King Hammurabi, and—like the Mitanni before them—clashed with the Egyptians, largely over the border town of Kadesh. In 1275 BCE a great battle was fought, which neither side really won. In 1272 BCE the Hittites signed a peace treaty with the Egyptians—the oldest known document of its kind. The Hittites were overthrown by the mysterious "Sea Peoples" in about 1196 BCE.

The Kassites

The Kassites were neither Indo-Europeans nor Semitic, and are thought to have come from the Zagros Mountains. The Hittites employed these nomadic warriors as mercenaries when they attacked Babylon. However, the Hittites never established themselves in Babylon, preferring to retire to the north, and the Kassites became the new rulers. They were eventually thrown out c.1150 BCE by the new great power in Mesopotamia—the Assyrians.

Celtic Tribes

Mycenaeans

GREECE

Hurrians also settle in Canaan

Egyptians

Nile

AFRICA

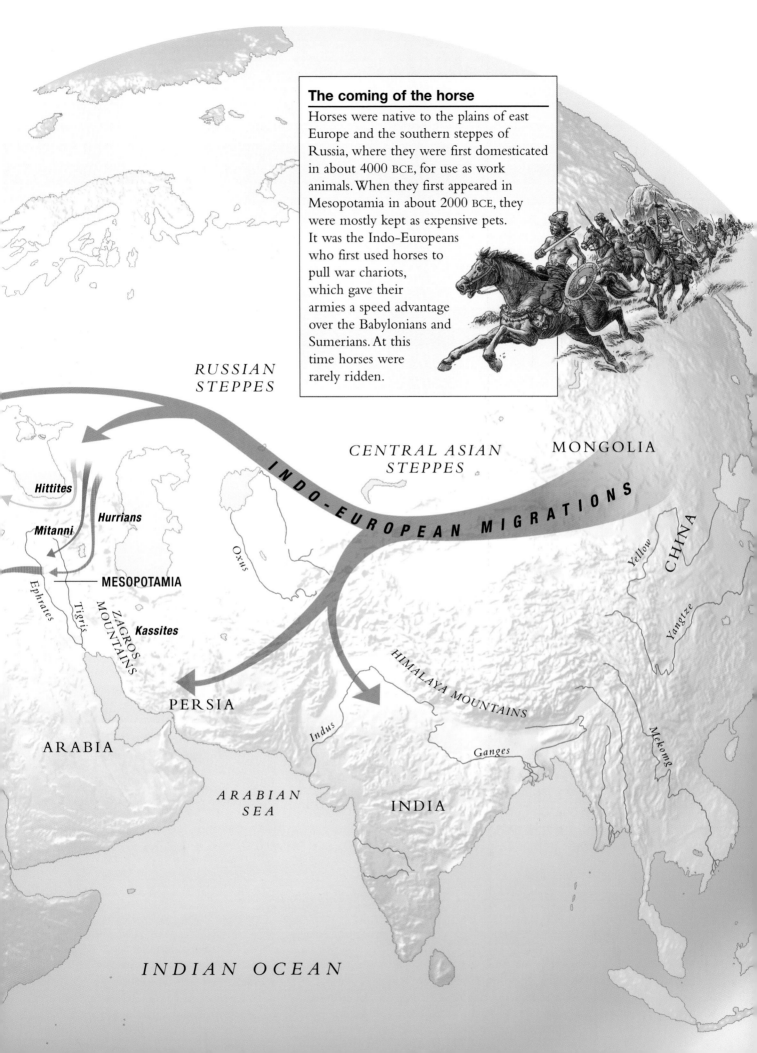

The coming of the horse

Horses were native to the plains of east Europe and the southern steppes of Russia, where they were first domesticated in about 4000 BCE, for use as work animals. When they first appeared in Mesopotamia in about 2000 BCE, they were mostly kept as expensive pets. It was the Indo-Europeans who first used horses to pull war chariots, which gave their armies a speed advantage over the Babylonians and Sumerians. At this time horses were rarely ridden.

RUSSIAN STEPPES

CENTRAL ASIAN STEPPES

MONGOLIA

INDO-EUROPEAN MIGRATIONS

Hittites

Hurrians

Mitanni

Oxus

CHINA

Yellow

MESOPOTAMIA

Euphrates

Tigris

ZAGROS MOUNTAINS

Kassites

Yangtze

HIMALAYA MOUNTAINS

PERSIA

Indus

Mekong

ARABIA

Ganges

ARABIAN SEA

INDIA

INDIAN OCEAN

The Rise and Fall of Assyria, 1420–609 BCE

The Assyrians are a Semitic speaking people who come to central Mesopotamia in about 3000 BCE. They are influenced culturally by their richer neighbors to the south in Sumer and Akkad, and at first are often under their political control as well.

The homeland of the Assyrians is a small region on the upper part of the Tigris, bounded by its tributaries the Great Zab and Little Zab. However, at some time before 2000 BCE, Semitic Amorites invade Assyria and establish a line of kings. By about 1800 BCE, the earliest known Assyrian rulers, Ishmi-Dagan and his son Shamshi-Adad I have united the cities of Ashur, Nineveh, and Arbil. Together with Nimrud, these cities form the core of Assyrian civilization.

Gaining independence

As late as the 15th century Assyria is still essentially a subject state. In 1472 BCE the Assyrian dominions are listed as being annexed to the Mitanni, and officials at the Assyrian court have Mitanni names. However, by 1420 royal inscriptions refer to Assyria as an independent state.

Under their kings the Assyrians build a huge empire, which reaches its greatest extent between 1000 and 612 BCE, the period known as the New Assyrian Empire.

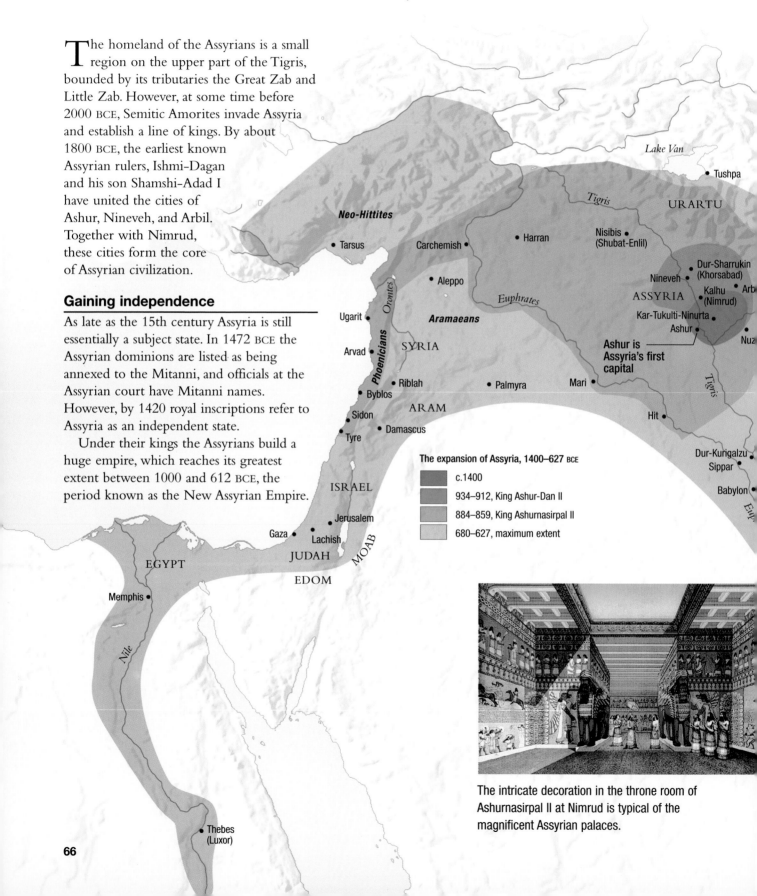

The expansion of Assyria, 1400–627 BCE

- c.1400
- 934–912, King Ashur-Dan II
- 884–859, King Ashurnasirpal II
- 680–627, maximum extent

Ashur is Assyria's first capital

The intricate decoration in the throne room of Ashurnasirpal II at Nimrud is typical of the magnificent Assyrian palaces.

Great engineers

The Assyrians are an aggressive military people, who make enemies among their neighbors as well as among their own subjects. With their formidable permanent army, the Assyrian kings usually win every battle, and their glory and successes are reflected in the magnificent palaces and cities they build. Among the most splendid are Khorsabad and Nimrud, decorated with painted stone carvings and monumental statues of winged bulls with the king's head (*see pages 78–79*).

The Assyrians' chief god is Ashur, after whom their main city is named. Like the Sumerians, the Assyrians build ziggurats for their gods, with large sacred precincts around them. They are also great builders of roads for the army and of aqueducts to bring water into the cities from the surrounding hillsides. Constructed of mud bricks, the aqueducts allow water to flow downhill through clay pipes waterproofed with a lining of bitumen (tar).

Statue of King Ashurnasirpal II

Medes

Diyala

Babylonia remains the religious and cultural center of the empire, despite Assyria's military dominance.

Susa

ABYLONIA

ELAM

ur

uk

Ur

Chaldeans

ancient coastline

Assyrian engineers are the first to build paved roads and span valleys with aqueducts to bring water to the cities.

Main dates (all BCE)

c.2000–1450 Old Assyrian Empire—dominated by Sumer and Akkad (Agade), Assyrians trade with Anatolia until Hittite expansion brings the relationship to an end, c.1500.

1813–1781 Reign of Shamshi-Adad I, who conquers an empire from Mari to Babylon. His son becomes a subject of Hammurabi in 1763.

c.1475 The Mitanni take control of Assyria.

1365–1329 Reign of Ashur-Uballit I, who regains Assyrian independence.

1273–1244 Reign of Shalmaneser I, who conquers the eastern part of the Mitanni kingdom.

1115–1077 Reign of Tiglath-Pileser I, who defeats the Mitanni and Kassites, and conquers Babylon, extending Assyrian influence into Syria and Armenia.

c.1000–612 New Assyrian Empire

884–859 Reign of Ashurnasirpal II, who moves the capital from Ashur to Nimrud, dedicated to the war god Ninurta, and populated with deported people from cities he captured.

858–824 Reign of Shalmaneser III, who conquers Israel. In the following years all of Palestine, Syria, Armenia, and Lower Mesopotamia are conquered.

727–722 Reign of Shalmaneser V, who subdues rebellious Israel and deports many Israelites to Mesopotamia.

721–705 Reign of Sargon III, who conquers Urartu and moves the capital to Khorsabad.

704–681 Reign of Sennacherib, who invades Egypt but withdraws and defeats Babylon.

668–627 Reign of Ashurbanipal II, who conquers Egypt and defeats Thebes in 663; in 648 he defeats Babylon, and Susa in 639.

614–612 Ashur and Nineveh are taken by Medes and Babylonians. By 608 Assyria ceases to exist.

Assyrian Society

The Assyrians are not a single race, but a nation of many different ethnic people, speaking a number of Semitic dialects. What unifies them is religion, centered on belief in a chief god named Ashur.

Surrounded by enemies from Sumer and Akkad in the south, mountain nomads from the east, and the Hittites to the north and west, the villagers of Assyria have become warriors. Now Assyria is the most feared power in Mesopotamia and the Fertile Crescent.

Many wall carvings depict warfare, but these are records of Assyrian achievements and victories rather than of everyday life. War is the task of the king and the land-owning nobles, but for ordinary folk, farming is their main occupation.

A farming economy

The Assyrians' economy is centered around their fields, crops, and livestock. A large part of the population consists of peasant farmers who are dependent on the land they own or land they are employed to cultivate. Unlike Sumer, Assyria is a nation of farming villages and country towns, with only a few large cities.

In the past, the land was owned by large families, who grouped together to form villages. These communities combined to undertake state projects, such as road building and digging irrigation canals. Now, in times of war, the villages provide manpower for military service. The people are bound to the land where they are born and where they labor. If the land is sold, they go with it.

Villages, towns, and cities

The village is administered by its local town, which has a court-appointed governor. His duties include acting as a judge in local disputes, collecting taxes for the king, and arranging festivals. The town in turn is responsible to one of the great cities that answer directly to the king.

In Assyria, every aspect of life is linked to the king, whose power is absolute. Unlike the Sumerian monarchs, the king is not a god, but his body emits a radiance that causes fear in his enemies on the battlefield. Anyone who wants to see the king—even the crown prince—must go through elaborate rites to make sure the omens are good before being granted an audience.

The king's palace is both the official royal residence and the seat of government, with a large administrative staff. As regent of the

For the majority of Assyrians, life is spent working on farms and rivers. This bas-relief carving shows ordinary folk going about their daily tasks, in this case harvesting grain and fishing in the Tigris.

Slaves haul a huge guardian statue up the bank to the city of Nineveh.

gods, the king must ensure that his actions accord with tradition and do not offend the gods. To help him, he is surrounded by a throng of priests, diviners, exorcists, and astrologers.

The king is always enlarging his capital city and adorning its buildings with huge statues and wall decorations made from colored, glazed tiles. The vast number of slaves captured in battle—or whole nations deported from their homelands—make this continual building work possible.

1. The River Tigris

2. The statue has been ferried from a quarry on a large raft.

3. The human-headed bull is moved off the raft and up the bank on a sled running on wooden rollers.

4. Slaves use a wooden lever wedged under the sled by large, constantly adjusted, wooden rollers.

5. Buckets of river water are passed up the slope by a chain gang of slaves to keep the track wet and lubricate the sled rollers.

6. Standing on the front of the sled, an officer clapping his hands in rhythm urges on the workers, while another shouts commands through a speaking horn.

7. Four chains of slaves haul on ropes to pull the 40-ton load up the slope. Each chain has a supervisor and a man armed with a whip to goad on the slackers.

The Assyrian Family

Assyrian society is decidedly patriarchal—the husband and father's word is law, and the rights and liberty of women is restricted in comparison to those of other Mesopotamians.

Assyrians have two indistinct social groups, free and non-free. Among the free citizens there are many subtle levels of status that reflect the wealth and influence of an individual. Non-free status, although generally meaning "slave," often indicates that the person is in a position of subservience to someone of higher authority.

The sons of poor families must report for military duty when required, while the sons of wealthy and noble families take up the duties of army officers. They might remain in a military career, or later become local or central government administrators.

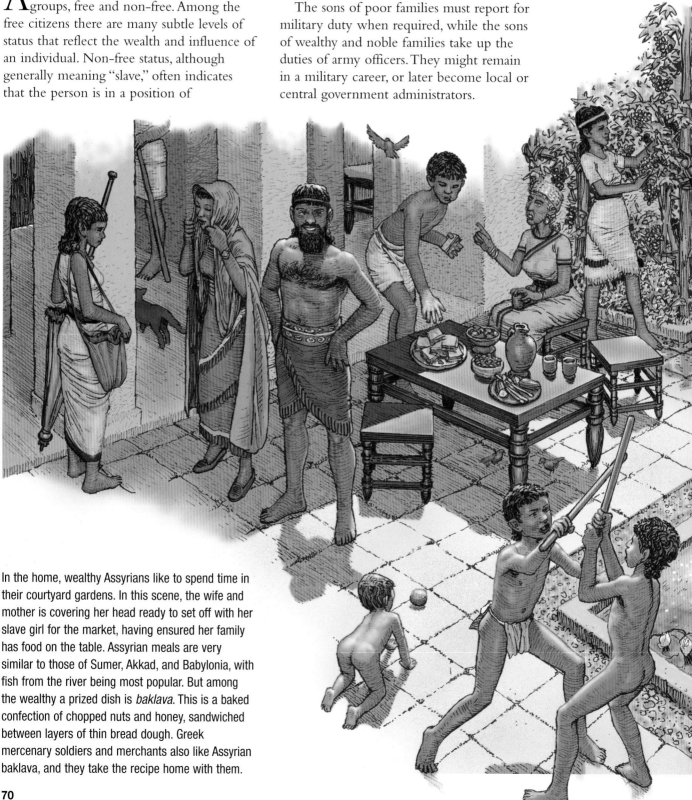

In the home, wealthy Assyrians like to spend time in their courtyard gardens. In this scene, the wife and mother is covering her head ready to set off with her slave girl for the market, having ensured her family has food on the table. Assyrian meals are very similar to those of Sumer, Akkad, and Babylonia, with fish from the river being most popular. But among the wealthy a prized dish is *baklava*. This is a baked confection of chopped nuts and honey, sandwiched between layers of thin bread dough. Greek mercenary soldiers and merchants also like Assyrian baklava, and they take the recipe home with them.

A man's property

In the privacy of their homes, both men and their wives go scantily clad, sometimes even naked. Outdoors, men generally wear a short tunic. An Assyrian nobleman usually has only one wife, but he is also allowed concubines —and, as a result, hopefully even more sons.

Women are under the authority of the male head of the family. A girl's father and future father-in-law arrange her marriage between them, and she has no say in the matter. After the wedding the bride comes under the authority of her husband as she moves to his household. As a wife, the girl has few property rights. Even jewelry given to her as a marriage gift becomes the property of her husband.

Girls are expected to marry early. They can legally be married as soon as they are ten, although the average age is 16. They are also encouraged to have many children— preferably boys to supply the king with soldiers for his armies. Women who bear sons are honored, while the husband may put aside a barren wife or even have her impaled on a stake.

A woman who is the "property" of an Assyrian nobleman—wife or daughter—is considered to be "respectable." (A widow comes under the authority of her eldest son.) Respectable women must cover their heads whenever they go out on the street. This is to distinguish them from "disreputable" women—prostitutes and slaves.

A concubine, or secondary wife, is also defined as respectable when she appears in public with the first wife, her mistress. But there are severe penalties for disreputable women caught wearing a head covering— 50 lashes for free women, and a slave has her ears cut off.

While a girl is getting married at about 16, her brother at the same age is starting his military service.

Funeral rites

Funeral rites in Assyria differ little from those of Sumer. In particular it is believed that the deceased belong inside the house they occupied while alive. In a poorer home, the body is buried in a small chamber under the stone floor, but larger homes have a special vaulted chamber, sealed off by a sturdy door that's reached through a steep shaft.

When his father dies, the eldest son performs the rites, reading a memorial service in front of the household's sacred niche. This contains an offering table and an opening in the wall occupied by the house god.

The master is removed from his deathbed and laid out ceremoniously on a stretcher to be taken to his grave. He's dressed in his finest robe, and his right hand laid on a vessel containing the food he will need in the afterlife. Along with him will go all his personal belongings— ornaments, weapons and armor, favorite vessels. In his death, the Assyrian nobleman remains the great warrior he was in life.

An Assyrian Soldier's Life

Assyrian boys start their military life at the age of 16. The Assyrians are the first people to employ a professional standing army. It's carefully organized and trained.

By 800 BCE, Assyria fields a vast army, with expert commanders and plentiful supplies of equipment for all types of combat. The regular army includes 20,000 infantry, 12,000 light cavalry armed with bows and spears, and 1,200 two-horse chariots. In the early days, the cavalry rode into action in chariots and dismounted to shoot arrows from behind wicker shields. Now the men ride their steeds and have mastered the art of firing from horseback at full gallop.

Right: A typical Assyrian mounted archer.

Kitted out with their basic equipment, raw recruits are herded toward their new life of order and rigor in the local military base, where they will be made into the efficient soldiers seen above.

The Assyrian military camp

Professional soldiers live on a military base, or *ekal masharti* (palace for marshalling forces) in the capital cities. The *ekal masharti* consists of a large courtyard for military maneuvers, surrounded by a number of buildings used as barracks and storerooms for provisions and equipment. Smaller garrisons are maintained at border crossings and other key points.

Conscripts supplement the regular army in times of foreign war. These forces are raised from within Assyria, but also from southern Mesopotamia by provincial governors, who are also responsible for providing provisions while the army is in their territory. By these means it is possible to field an army of as many as 200,000 men.

The aristocratic recruit

In whichever division the new recruit finds himself, he is under the unit's commander, the intelligence officers, interpreters, and a diviner who foretells events.

Depending on his skills in general training, he might be placed in the pioneer corps, responsible for road building in difficult terrain and for constructing rafts and bridges when they are needed. Or, if he's nobly-born, he might get promoted to the elite royal bodyguard that provides personal security for the king.

The ordinary soldier

Poorer recruits form the bulk of the army—bowmen, slingsmen, swordsmen, pike-bearers, and light and heavy infantry, as well as permanent units of charioteers and cavalry. There's also a section that deals only with the transport of military equipment and basic provisions (mainly corn and oil). These are carried on pack-donkeys or on carts drawn by teams of oxen.

Among the equipment to be transported are armored battering rams, large wheeled machines that provide sufficient cover for several men to operate the ram, which is suspended from heavy chains so that it can be swung back and forth.

This detail from a relief (**below right**) shows a scene of cruelty after Sennacherib's assault on the Judaean city of Lachish, c.681 BCE. Captured prisoners are impaled on stakes. Carved scenes like this adorn the walls of the king's audience chamber—a warning to foreign ambassadors not to mess with Assyria.

Battles of body and mind

There are distinct war seasons, sanctioned by the war god Ninurta, that follow harvesting in July. This is a time when peasant labor is available for military service.

When the Assyrians surround an enemy town, the soldiers shout at the defenders to surrender. They proclaim that their gods have predicted victory and that resistance will be useless. If this form of psychological warfare fails to impress the enemy, a siege is made. A fortified camp is set up outside the town, and its food and water supplies are cut. When the town's people are sufficiently weakened, the battering rams are brought into play or the walls are scaled.

Psychological warfare is also employed after a victory, when the flayed skins of the enemy's leaders are publicly displayed to discourage others from rebelling. Other punishments may include the severing of hands, putting out of eyes, and the cutting off of noses and ears. However, the usual punishment for prisoners is deportation to a distant part of the empire, where they will be less likely to cause further trouble.

Forced Migrations

To Assyria's neighbors its most upsetting military policy is the mass deportation of subject peoples. Scholars often describe this policy as inhumane, yet it is important to consider it from the Assyrian point of view.

Numerous surrounding small tribes and alliances frequently challenge the rule of the king. Although the Assyrian army is capable of suppressing such uprisings, it cannot guarantee that they will not happen again. Therefore, stability of the Assyrian way of life depends on relocating populations in less troubled regions and by destroying the rule of their feudal lords.

It is not a punishment

There are also good economic reasons for the relocations. As the empire gains more territory, it needs more crops to feed the extra people, and this means making better use of agricultural lands. Who better to populate unproductive areas than those captured in war?

Other prisoners are settled in cities where their craft skills can be employed, and some are given high-status positions within the Assyrian court as scribes and interpreters. It is sometimes suggested that these relocations are intended to be a punishment, but in fact they are carefully planned movements intended to place new populations in areas where their skills can be most usefully employed.

Supply and demand

This is a time when relocation of entire populations by migration is common, and so being forcibly moved is not as upsetting as it would be today.

The deported people are sent to settle in places similar to those they came from, and they are looked after. These are not forced marches in shackles and chains, but well supervised movements during which the comfort and health of the people is important. In fact they are often better clothed and better fed than many rural Assyrian families.

In the countryside, the resettled populations work alongside existing rural villagers and they have the same rights and obligations as anyone else. New immigrants are provided for by the state until they can settle themselves in their new homes, and state officials are appointed to oversee any problems of integration with the local populace.

The Assyrians do not break up ethnic groups or separate family members, and all deportees remain technically free persons, able to follow their own religious beliefs and speak their own language. All they are expected to do is express their loyalty to Ashur.

Enriching Assyrian society

In contrast to making war, the Assyrians enjoy the cultural mix they have created through the deportations. Ethnic differences are not important to them, and they do not see racial purity as relevant. Indeed, the king likes to boast of the number of languages spoken at court and that all people, of whatever ethnic group, background, or culture, are equal.

Many of the leading craftsmen in cities such as Nineveh are foreign, as are some of the most important architects. People from outside Assyria constantly add to the mix of nations that are represented in these cosmopolitan cities. Even the Assyrian language has changed dramatically as words from other cultures are accepted.

An Assyrian army batters its way into a rebel city.

Far left: In the siege of the Syrian city of Hamath, the defenders are seen on the ramparts, some falling after being struck by arrows. Assyrian soldiers shelter under shields, some attack with a ladder, others make a sneak attack by swimming in the River Orontes.

Left: A city's population begins its deportation to a foreign land for resettlement, under Assyrian guard.

The Jews in exile

This issue of Assyrian deportations is emotive, mostly because it is linked in the Bible with the deportation of the "Ten Tribes of Israel" from Samaria in 722–720 BCE during the reigns of Shalmaneser V (727–722) and Sargon II (721–705). It was carried out on a vast scale during the reign of Sennacherib (704–681), who is said to have deported 20,000 inhabitants of the city of Judah, and continued under Esarhaddon (681–669).

Hunting—the Sport of Kings

Although hunting in Mesopotamia is a means of providing extra food, in Assyria it has a greater significance as a ritual act performed by the king. Through hunting, he demonstrates his power over the wild beasts of the land.

Right: King Ashurbanipal confronts his "divine" opponent, the lion. Armed attendants ensure the king comes to no harm. Due to continual hunting by Assyrian kings, the Assyrian lion is now extinct.

Ritual hunting has long been a sport of the Assyrian kings, as the records show. We are told that Tiglath-Pileser I (1115–1077 BCE) enjoyed hunting many different types of beast—bear, hyena, lion, tiger, leopard, deer, wild goat, bison, water buffalo, wild pig, gazelle, wild sheep, lynx, cheetah, wild ass (onager), wild ox, elephant, and even ostrich.

When Tiglath-Pileser visited the Mediterranean city of Arvad, he commandeered a boat and harpooned a *nahiru* (sea-horse, but it was probably a dolphin or some species of whale) while at sea. Knowing the king's fascination with wild animals, and particularly foreign species, many ambassadors to the court make gifts of these. Although some are later hunted, most of these strange specimens are kept in several large zoos—animals such as apes, crocodiles, and other oddities captured in the Syrian Desert.

A mass slaying

The royal hunts are no mere day-out affairs. Large numbers of animals are killed for sport. Tiglath-Pileser claims to have killed up to 800 lions at a time, and Ashurnasirpal II (884–859) claims that "Ninurta and Nergal [gods of war and the hunt], who love my priesthood, gave me the wild animals of the plains, commanding me to hunt. Thirty elephants I trapped and killed; 257 great wild oxen I brought down with my weapons, attacking from my chariot; 370 great lions I killed with my hunting spears."

The king believes the "great beasts" are divine and his alone to hunt as a display of his power. Lions are trapped and brought in cages to a hunting arena, where they are released and set on by his soldiers and trained mastiffs.

The king's own role is mostly a ritual one—he only steps in at the last moment to finish off the lion with a spear or dagger. Even then, trained archers are always standing by, ready to ensure that the king comes to no harm.

Sometimes there are practical reasons beyond sport for a hunt. It is the king's duty

to protect his subjects from attack by wild animals. An unusually rainy period can trigger an increase in the lion population, and then they attack the livestock and farmers with terrible consequences.

On the other hand, in drier years the king's hunting can deplete the wild livestock so much that his hunt masters are forced to import lions, leopards, and gazelles from Africa. Lions are also bred at zoos specifically to be released into the enclosures for ritual hunts.

Cities of Splendor and Learning

Between the 9th and 7th centuries BCE, Assyria's main urban centers are among the most splendid cities anywhere, each in its time the capital of a great king. Nineveh contains the finest library in the world.

The Assyrian kings built magnificent palace-cities such as Nineveh (**above**), located on the River Khasr, on the east bank of the Tigris.

Center right: A carved relief from Sargon's palace at Dur-Sharrukin (Khorsabad).

Right: A look inside Ashurbanipal's vast library complex.

Far right: Reconstruction of Sargon's palace at Dur-Sharrukin. The complex was never completed.

Nineveh

Nineveh is an ancient place, once occupied by the kings of Agade (2300 BCE), then Shamshi-Adad of Ashur (1800 BCE), and later by the Mitanni. Since 1000 BCE it has been the main Assyrian royal city.

The walls of Sennacherib are about 50 feet high and enclose an area 7.5 miles around. The city has 15 gates for access, each named after an Assyrian god and flanked by winged bulls with human heads. At the center, Sennacherib's palace stands on top of Tell Kuyunjik. It covers nearly 10 acres and contains at least 80 rooms decorated with stone reliefs and wall paintings.

Nineveh has many public squares and parks, wide boulevards, a botanical garden, and a zoo. The oldest known aqueduct brings water from hills 30 miles away to irrigate exotic plants and trees in the parks and gardens. So great is the city that its suburbs extend almost 30 miles along the river's bank.

Ashurbanipal's fabulous library

A second palace on Kuyunjik belongs to Ashurbanipal II, who is also responsible for construction of the state library. This astonishing building contains between 20,000 and 30,000 clay tablets, gathered from many countries. The tablets are organized in several rooms arranged according to subject matter—history/government, religion/magic, geography, science, and poetry.

The library's contents include "books" that foretell the future, translations of Sumerian and Akkadian stories, religious incantations, instruction manuals for priests in training, and legal documents. There are also books of poetry, proverbs, myths, and epics, including the *Epic of Gilgamesh*.

Proud of his library, Ashurbanipal fearsomely warns any who misbehave: "May all the gods curse anyone who breaks, defaces, or removes this tablet…and may they put his flesh in a dog's mouth."

Nimrud

Founded by Shalmaneser I (1273–1244), Nimrud also sits on the east bank of the Tigris, not far from Nineveh. Ashurnasirpal II (884–859) made it his capital. The inner city covers about 500 acres, surrounding the major buildings at its southwest corner. These include a temple dedicated to the city's patron god Ninurta, with a large ziggurat. Nimrud also has extensive orchards and parks, all drained by a clever sewage system.

Ashurnasirpal's palace is decorated with numerous plaster reliefs and wall paintings, and colossal winged lions and bulls flank the doorways. When the king held a feast for the builders and architects who had worked on it, he fed 63,000 people, including 47,000 workers who had been brought there from conquered lands.

Dur-Sharrukin (modern Khorsabad)

This capital was purpose-built by Sargon II (721–705) but lasted for only his reign. With each wall about a mile long, the city is almost a square. Seven gates lead through high fortified walls into the inner city, which contains a second wall surrounding the Palace of Sargon to the northwest. This stands on a great terrace, about 46 feet high, and straddles the exterior wall. The palace precinct has a large temple and ziggurat, a harem for the king's four wives, a kitchen, bakery, and wine cellar.

There are many carved stone reliefs lining the palace walls, and massive statues of Sargon and winged bulls. Among the carvings are scenes of military campaigns, everyday life, rituals, ceremonies, and lavish banquets like the one below, showing Sargon reclining, celebrating a victory.

CHAPTER 4
NEW BABYLONIA

The Glory of Nebuchadnezzar's City

Assyria collapsed after the death of Ashurbanipal and Babylon declared its independence. Under its first two Chaldean rulers, Nabopolassar and his son Nebuchadnezzar II, Babylon has become the greatest city in Mesopotamia.

With Assyria crushed and Nineveh razed to the ground, Babylon has at last the opportunity to regain the prominence it enjoyed more than a thousand years before, during the golden age of Hammurabi. Its hopes are realized under the long and able rule of Nabopolassar's son, Nebuchadnezzar.

Nebuchadnezzar II (605–562 BCE) claims royal descent from his ancestor, the Akkadian king Naram-Sin. In addition to his royal duties, he is also a high priest of Marduk (*see pages 88–89*) and the god's son, Nebu—in fact Nebuchadnezzar means "Nebu will protect me."

The largest city in the world

Years of internal strife and many wars have left much of the country's farm land neglected and its temples in ruins. Nebuchadnezzar has now restored more than 40 temples in major cities such as Borsippa, Sippar, Ur, Uruk, Larsa, Dilbat, and Baz. He has also completely overhauled the canal system and built a major new canal that connects the Euphrates to the Tigris.

Under his rule, Babylonia is again the most important economic and military power of Mesopotamia, and Babylon has become its most glorious city.

The Greek writer Herodotus claims that Babylon is the largest and most splendid city in the known world. He says that the outer walls are 56 miles long, 80 feet thick and almost 330 feet high. Herodotus says that the road on the top of the wall is wide enough for a four-horse chariot to turn, and that a moat 164 feet across surrounds the city.

Herodotus exaggerates

Perhaps the Greeks have not yet mastered Sumerian arithmetic—the moat is actually 39 feet wide, and there are three fortified walls around the city. However, the real statistics are still impressive. The outer wall, beyond the moat, is 23 feet thick and the space between the two inner walls is wide enough to act as a military road. The inner wall (18 feet thick) is further reinforced with towers at 59-foot intervals, with eight gates and drawbridges leading into the city itself. This wall stretches for 11 miles.

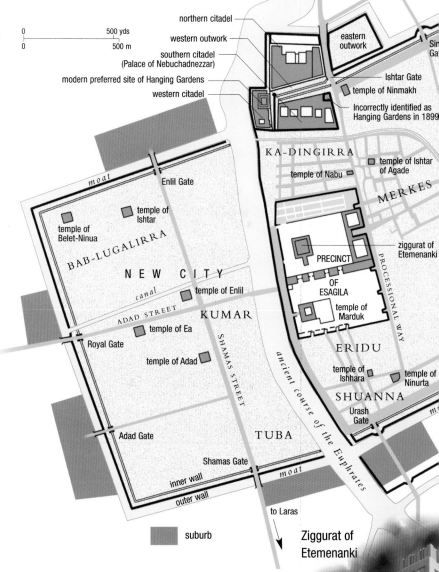

Ziggurat of Etemenanki

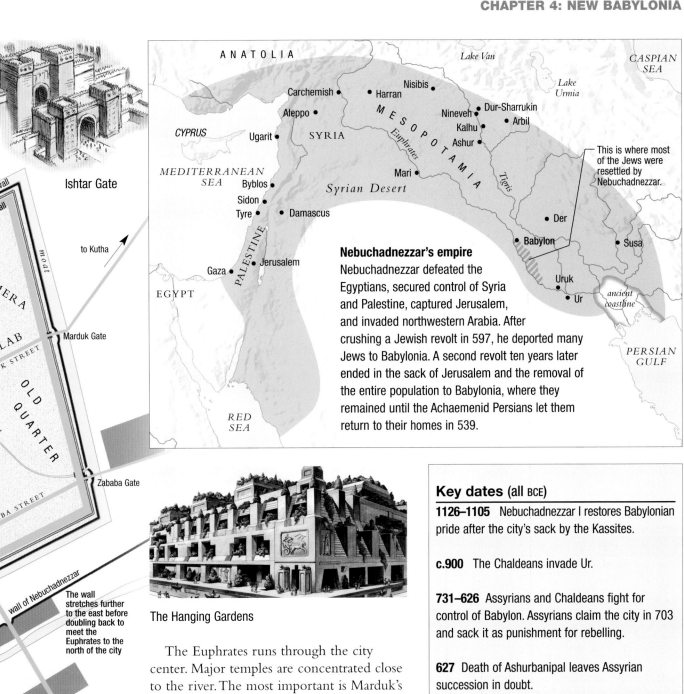

Ishtar Gate

to Kutha

Marduk Gate

OLD QUARTER

Zababa Gate

wall of Nebuchadnezzar

The wall stretches further to the east before doubling back to meet the Euphrates to the north of the city

to Nippur

ANATOLIA

Lake Van

CASPIAN SEA

Lake Urmia

Carchemish

Harran

Nisibis

Nineveh

Dur-Sharrukin

Aleppo

Kalhu

Arbil

MESOPOTAMIA

CYPRUS

Ugarit

SYRIA

Ashur

Euphrates

Tigris

This is where most of the Jews were resettled by Nebuchadnezzar.

MEDITERRANEAN SEA

Byblos

Mari

Syrian Desert

Sidon

Tyre

Damascus

Der

Babylon

Susa

PALESTINE

Jerusalem

Gaza

EGYPT

Uruk

Ur

ancient coastline

PERSIAN GULF

RED SEA

Nebuchadnezzar's empire

Nebuchadnezzar defeated the Egyptians, secured control of Syria and Palestine, captured Jerusalem, and invaded northwestern Arabia. After crushing a Jewish revolt in 597, he deported many Jews to Babylonia. A second revolt ten years later ended in the sack of Jerusalem and the removal of the entire population to Babylonia, where they remained until the Achaemenid Persians let them return to their homes in 539.

The Hanging Gardens

The Euphrates runs through the city center. Major temples are concentrated close to the river. The most important is Marduk's temple of Esagila and its ziggurat of Etemenanki (*see pages 90–91*).

The glory of New Babylon

Nebuchadnezzar's palace is magnificent. It has more than 600 rooms, whose brick walls are inscribed with Nebuchadnezzar's name as the protector of Babylonia. In these rooms there are gold and lapis lazuli-encrusted sculptures and carvings made by the best craftsmen of the city. His architects are also responsible for one of the world's greatest architectural masterpieces: the Hanging Gardens of Babylon.

Key dates (all BCE)

1126–1105 Nebuchadnezzar I restores Babylonian pride after the city's sack by the Kassites.

c.900 The Chaldeans invade Ur.

731–626 Assyrians and Chaldeans fight for control of Babylon. Assyrians claim the city in 703 and sack it as punishment for rebelling.

627 Death of Ashurbanipal leaves Assyrian succession in doubt.

630–605 Nabopolassar, governor of Babylon, declares independence from Assyria. **614**, he marries his son Nebuchadnezzar to Amytis, daughter of Umakishtar, uniting the Chaldeans and Persian Medes.

626–539 Neo Babylonian Empire under Nabopolassar, Nebuchadnezzar II, Merodach (561–60), Neriglissar (559–56), and Nabonidus (556–39).

539 The Achaemenid Persian Cyrus II conquers the empire of Babylonia.

A Society Run by Priests

As in most other cities of Mesopotamia, distinct class divisions exist, especially between slaves and the free citizens. In Babylon there is also a great divide between the temple priests and the ordinary people.

Nebuchadnezzar's new Babylon sits astride the Euphrates, with the old quarter on the east bank and an entire new city on the west bank. There are ten districts (*see the map, page 80*) separate from the temple precinct of Esagila and the royal palace. The space within the walls is packed with houses; as many as 200,000 people live here.

The population is very mixed, reflecting the history of conquerors and conquered. Native Babylonians mingle with Aramaeans, Assyrians, Chaldeans, Egyptians, Elamites, Hittites, Hurrians, Kassites, and now thousands of Jews deported from Jerusalem by Nebuchadnezzar.

The wealthy temple priests

The temples form a virtual state within a state. The only formal education takes place at them and is reserved for those preparing to enter temple service or be part of the royal court. The priests of Marduk at the Esagila precinct are the biggest owners of land and real estate, with half of Babylon under their direct control. The authority of their

senior representatives rivals that of the king. They also have vast business interests and own a sizable part of Babylon's shipping fleet.

This means that the priests control the lives of all kinds of traders and craftsmen. Thousands of farmers work the temple lands for a share of its produce. Agricultural workers might be slaves or paid laborers, but some can also be captured soldiers who have no citizens' rights but remain free men.

The high priestly status

The priests also own thousands of slaves who make up the work gangs that maintain the city's many canals. The canals are essential for irrigation of the fields and are useful for shipping goods to and fro.

Temple and court officials live within the temple and palace precincts, where special quarters are reserved for them according to

1. The Ziggurat of Etemenanki (the Biblical "Tower of Babel")

2. Processional avenue from the Ishtar Gate to the religious precincts

3. Northern Precinct of Esagila

4. Western arm of processional avenue leading to the bridge

5. Southern Precinct of Esagila with priests' quarters and stores

6. Temple of Marduk, chief god of Babylon

7. Bridge crossing the Euphrates to the New City on the west bank

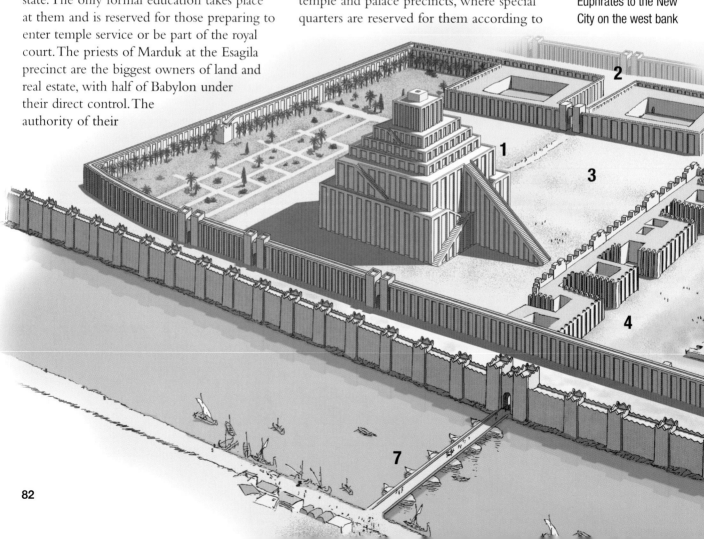

their status and the duties they perform. These precincts also house most of the military and provide accommodation for visiting diplomats and officials.

Many aristocrats prefer temple life, with its rich financial rewards and social prestige, but others make a career in the highest levels of the military.

Babylonia's wealthy class

Most wealthy Babylonians are either owners of large farm estates, or they control trading or manufacturing companies with large, paid workforces. There are many trade guilds for master craftsmen and apprentices. These include boatmen, brewers, brick-makers, canal-diggers, confectioners, coppersmiths, fowlers, leatherworkers, and many others.

The choice of profession is limited because a man follows the trade of his father, unless there are special circumstances, such as the son being especially gifted in a different skill from that of his father.

Life of a slave

Temple slaves work hard, every day, but for others being a slave does not necessarily mean suffering. The living standard of a slave in a wealthy household is much higher than a poor but free citizen enjoys. Male slaves usually do much of the manual labor, and

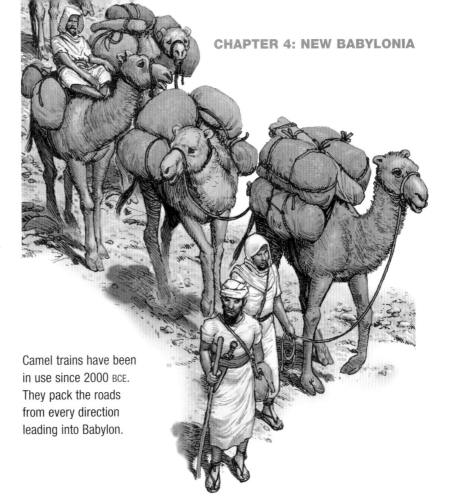

Camel trains have been in use since 2000 BCE. They pack the roads from every direction leading into Babylon.

Dignitaries of subject states make their way toward the royal palace to attend a celebratory feast with the king. This carved relief is from the stepped wall of a walkway.

their duties depend on their owner's profession.

Young female slaves are employed as maids to the lady of the house, and sometimes as concubines of the owner or one of his teenage sons. When older, they take over duties such as grinding corn, collecting water, house-keeping, and cooking.

Daily Life in Babylon—Home and Festival

New Babylon is a devoutly religious city. Apart from its many temple complexes, there are small altars on the approaches to temples, at each of the city gates, at crossroads, and in the home, where prayers can be offered.

Babylonians treasure their privacy, and most homes are built around an enclosed courtyard with only a single door opening onto the street. Apart from the temple and court officials, homes are distinguished by size, more prosperous families having more and larger rooms than the less well off.

Most homes are single story, with blank outer walls up to 6.5 feet thick to protect against the heat of the sun. The entrance doorway opens onto the inner courtyard, around which are arranged the living rooms, bedrooms, and slave quarters. On the north side of the house a large room serves as a kitchen, with a bathroom at the south fitted with a drain.

The family's day

Babylonians bathe every day. Standing over the drain, each family member in turn is doused with water from a bowl held over them by a slave. A brisk rub down follows, and the application of olive oil and perfume.

The family rises early to make the most of the daylight hours, and dawn finds the men and boys already bathed and dressed and on the rooftop, bowing on their knees to the rising sun. With prayers over, everyone goes down to a big breakfast.

Depending on the family's profession, the day might be spent attending to business in various parts of the city, but it will certainly include making routine sacrifices at one of the numerous small temples. The family reassembles for a light luncheon, followed by a siesta during the hot early afternoon. Work continues until almost dusk, when everyone returns home for the second main meal.

The Sacred Marriage

As in the past eras of Mesopotamia, many festivals happen throughout the year, but the most important is that of the New Year held in the spring. It lasts for the first 11 days of Nisannu, meaning "first [month]". At the

Plan showing a Babylonian house and its courtyards.

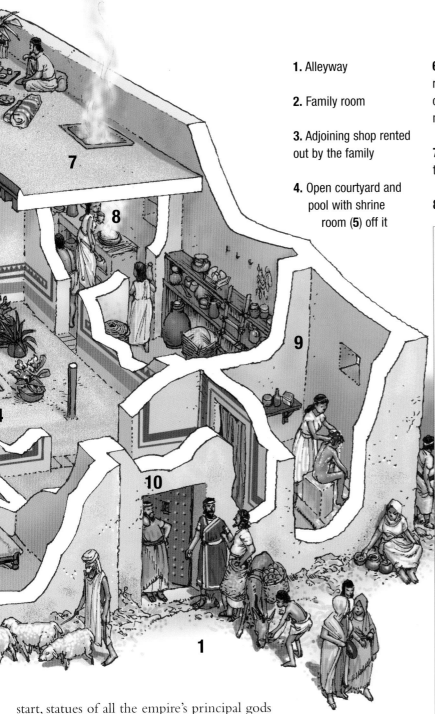

1. Alleyway

2. Family room

3. Adjoining shop rented out by the family

4. Open courtyard and pool with shrine room (**5**) off it

6. Stairs up to the flat roof, where the family often takes the evening meal in the cooling air

7. Smoke outlet from the kitchen

8. Kitchen

9. Bathroom, with central drain

10. Entrance and doorway to the house

11. Various bedrooms

12. Slave quarters

A substitute king stays on to rule

The concluding custom of the New Year festival, Mock King-for-a-Day, has survived since the earliest times. In the mists of time it was believed that the king's highest duty to his people was to sacrifice himself to the gods at the New Year, and thus make way for a new king for a year. In time this inconvenient and wasteful practice was replaced by selecting an expendable substitute king for the day to stand in for the real king.

The person selected for this unwanted privilege of appeasing the gods by paying with his life for brief occupancy of the throne, is usually a prisoner. However, on at least one occasion in the days of Old Babylonia, things went wrong—or right, depending on how you look at it.

King Erra-Imitti of Isin (early second millennium BCE) set up a gardener named Enlil-Bani as substitute ruler. After the crown had been placed on his head it was discovered that Erra-Imitti had died in his palace. Enlil-Bani ended up keeping not only his life but the crown as well. This rare prank of fate left Enlil-Bani on the throne for no less than 24 years and—mock king or not—he proved to be a very capable ruler.

start, statues of all the empire's principal gods are assembled in the precinct of Esagila. They are then moved with solemn ceremony and in strict order of divine precedence from the temple, along the procession street, through the Gate of Ishtar to the northern suburbs. Here they are transferred to boats and taken to the garden temple up the river.

Then follows the central part of the festival, the sacred marriage of the principal god and goddess, Marduk and Inanna, on which depends the fertility and prosperity of the whole land. On the eleventh day of Nissanu the procession joyously returns to the city through the Ishtar Gate, the gods now placed in "carriage boats."

The Hanging Gardens

Just inside the Ishtar Gate visitors are dazzled by one of the Seven Wonders of the World—the Hanging Gardens of Babylon. In the blazing desert heat of the city, throngs gaze up in wonder at the man-made mountain of greenery.

Amytis, daughter of the Medean king Umakishtar and Nebuchadnezzar II's favorite wife, found the sun-baked terrain of Mesopotamia depressing—she pined for the trees and hills of her northern homeland. And so Nebuchadnezzar had these gardens built for her enjoyment. They consist of a series of irrigated terraces said to be several hundred feet high (*see "Fable or reality?"*), planted with trees of all description.

The use of rare stone

The gardens are an amazing feat of engineering. Water is raised from the nearby Euphrates, collected in a pool on the top terrace, and then released through a series of small dams into the terraces below. Each terrace is many feet in depth to accommodate the roots of fully grown trees.

The main construction, as usual in Mesopotamia, is of mud brick, which deteriorates rapidly in wet conditions. To prevent them from dissolving from the continual irrigation, each terrace platform consists of huge slabs of costly, imported stone. These are covered with layers of reed, asphalt, and baked clay tiles. Over this the architects placed a covering of lead sheets to prevent the foundation from rotting.

Watering the gardens

The ascent to the highest story is by stairs, and at their side are water engines that lift water from the Euphrates into the garden. The engines are chain pumps—two large wheels, one above the other, connected by a chain, on which hang buckets. Slaves operate the pumps, all day long. As the wheels are turned, the buckets at the bottom dip into a pool fed by the river and pick up water. The chain then lifts them to the upper wheel, where the buckets are tipped and their contents dumped into an upper cistern. The water then flows into channels through gates to water the gardens.

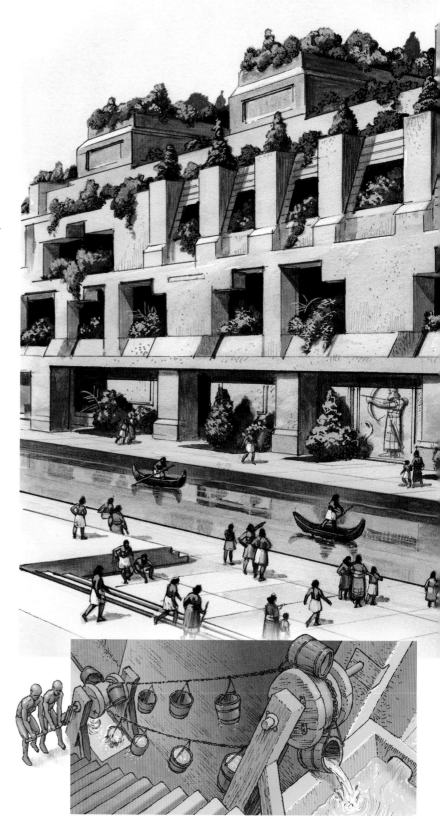

Fable or reality?

The location, height, and size of the Hanging Gardens remain a mystery. Indeed, some archaeologists even doubt they ever existed. The famous Greek geographer Strabo (1st century BCE) says the gardens are "vaulted terraces raised one above another, and resting on cube-shaped pillars. These are hollow and filled with earth to allow trees of the largest size to be planted."

His contemporary Diodorus Siculus claims the gardens are about 400 feet wide by 400 feet long and more than 80 feet high. Unfortunately, Herodotus, chronicler and exaggerator of Babylon's palaces, canals, and fortifications, makes no mention of the gardens.

Modern archaeologists have been unable to locate them with certainty. In 1899 CE, German archaeologist Robert Koldewey discovered a basement close to the Ishtar Gate with 14 vaulted brick-built chambers. He declared this to be the site of the gardens, but modern archaeologists think this wrong and that the Hanging Gardens were sited on the river bank, just above the western citadel.

Left: How water from the River Euphrates is hoisted up to cisterns, from which the gardens are irrigated.

The God Marduk

In later Mesopotamian culture Marduk exists in many forms, with as many as 50 different names. His presence as the chief Babylonian deity is central to the Chaldean civilization.

Every New Year the god Marduk returns to Babylon and, accompanied by a procession of sacred boats, passes through the Ishtar Gate, on his way to the great ziggurat of Etemenanki, atop which sits his temple. From there he dispenses his blessings on the land and people.

Marduk's name means "bull calf of the sun," and he is sometimes portrayed as a double-headed sun. The sacred texts tell us that Marduk is the son of Enki (called Ea by the Chaldeans) and the Babylonian successor to the Sumerian god Enlil, son of An and Ki (*see page 44*). He assumed the leadership of the Sumerian gods during the struggle with Tiamat (*see page 60*).

Having won his victory over Chaos, Marduk informed the divine assembly that henceforward Babylon would be the center of the cosmic universe, and there he built himself a luxurious house. He came to be known to the people as Bel, which simply means "Lord." To approach his house and worship Marduk, the people had to pass through his gate, which in the Babylonian/Assyrian tongue is Bab-ili, or "Gate of God."

And so the place became known as Babel, the original name of Babylon.

The spread of Marduk's worship

Marduk's cult first rose to prominence during the reign of Hammurabi, whose conquests spread the god's name throughout Mesopotamia. The Assyrians accepted Marduk but regarded Ashur as more worthy of worship. Nevertheless, Assyria's conquests of Mediterranean coastal territories brought Marduk to Phoenicia, Canaan, and Israel.

His worship in these areas has been cemented by Nebuchadnezzar's rule over them. In Phoenicia, Canaan, and Israel Marduk is worshipped as Bel, which they pronounce Baal (*see "Fact box"*).

Marduk's son is Nebu, whose sign is the planet Mercury. He is the patron of writing and his job is to inscribe the laws and commands of his father and then communicate them to men. His shrine is at Borsippa but, like all the other principal gods, Nebu is ceremoniously carried at the New Year to join Marduk in Babylon.

Great Etemenanki

In Babylon, Marduk resides on top of the great ziggurat Etemenanki. The name *E-temen-an-ki* means "House of the foundation of Heaven on Earth," and is the place where Marduk first descended to Earth after his victory over Tiamat.

This is the most sacred place in Babylonia, where Marduk returns every New Year to renew the people's faith and ensure the fertility and prosperity of the country by his marriage to Innana. There has been a ziggurat here for a thousand or more years, but never as grand or tall as that built by Nebuchadnezzar.

God confounds the people

In the Bible, according to the *Book of Genesis*, after the Great Flood Noah's descendants founded a city and attempted to build a tower whose top would reach Heaven. For their presumption to equal his divine power, God sent winds to topple the "Tower of Babel" and scatter the people. As at the time they all spoke the same tongue, he also confused their languages so that they could no longer understand one another.

This story in *Genesis* refers to the ziggurat Etemenanki—the Tower of Babel, or Babylon. There are links between the biblical story and Mesopotamian records. According to Nebuchadnezzar's inscriptions, Etemenanki was made so that "its top might rival Heaven." And Babylon is indeed abuzz with many different languages.

Nebuchadnezzar tells us that he has called on "various peoples...from the mountains and the coasts" to help with its construction. Many of them are people from conquered nations, such as Israel, who have been relocated in Babylon to serve as a labor force during the king's rebuilding programs.

Mesopotamian fact and legend is now woven into Jewish history.

The Tower of Babel

The great ziggurat of Etemenanki in the precinct of Esagila, dedicated to Marduk, soars above the bustling wharves of Nebuchadnezzar's capital on the Euphrates.

The ziggurat of Etemenanki—built on the site of many previous shrines to Marduk—was begun by Nabopolassar and completed during the reign of Nebuchadnezzar II. The New City on the west bank of the Euphrates is connected to the temple precinct of Esagila by a bridge supported on piers of baked brick coated with asphalt, faced with stone. Its construction across the deep and fast-flowing Euphrates is an engineering feat in itself, but the ziggurat dwarfs it.

Millions of bricks

As with other Mesopotamian ziggurats, Etemenanki is not built from stone, which is rare in the region. It is constructed from trodden clay with a 50-foot-thick outer covering of millions of sun-dried mud and straw bricks, with bitumen as mortar to hold them together.

In the arid conditions of the Mesopotamian plain, such a structure is relatively stable; however, it can be damaged by water, which softens the bricks and causes them to crumble. Therefore, the architects have incorporated elaborate drainage systems, and slave gangs provide regular maintenance and periodic rebuilding.

Seven banded levels

The Etemenanki ziggurat has seven stages, connected by stairways that alternate along each side at the different levels, so climbing to the top requires the visitor to make a complete circuit of the building. The height of the seven stages is 298.5 feet, the same measurement as for each side of the square base.

Each stage is a different color. From base to top these are white, white, red, bronze, silver, gold, and blue. At its summit, the sanctuary's exterior is covered with blue glazed tiles. The interior has a cedar roof and walls plated with gold and embellished with alabaster and lapis lazuli. Inside is an altar with a solid gold statue of Marduk seated on a golden throne, together with a gold couch and footstool.

Stairway to Heaven

Nebuchadnezzar has given the people the clearest sign of the gods' favor and brought Mesopotamian civilization to its peak. Viewed by the visitor from the triple gate, the doorways on the higher terraces seem to be standing on top of each other and Etemenanki resembles a true "stairway to Heaven."

Fact box

In the Hebrew language "babel" means to "confuse."

The English word "babble," meaning to chatter, prattle, or speak confusingly, is derived from Babel, where God confused the languages of all the people.

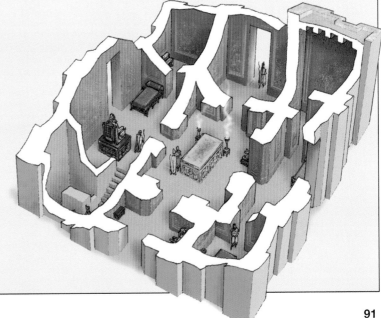

The Shrine of Marduk

The sanctuary on the top level has several rooms. Marduk shares his room with his consort Sarpanitum, mother of the scribe-god Nebu, who shares his room with his wife Tashmetu. There are rooms for the water god Ea (Enki), the god of fire and light Nusku, the god of Heaven Anu, and finally Enlil, Marduk's predecessor as chief of the Mesopotamian gods.

Achaemenids, Seleucids, Arsacids, and Sassanids

Ancient Mesopotamia's most glorious time under the Chaldean Babylonians is short-lived. Nebuchadnezzar's firm rule has not been matched by his successors, who pass in a few years. Their weakness leaves Babylonia open to invasion.

Stela of Nabodinus, last of the Neo-Babylonian kings, who made the Assyrian moon god Sin more powerful than Marduk.

The reconstruction of Persepolis shows the scale of the massive city-palace of the Achaemenid kings after the capital was moved from nearby Pasargadae. It was burned to the ground by Alexander the Great.

A unfinished gate
B outbuildings and storerooms
C Hall of 100 Columns
D east gate
E tomb of Artaxerxes
F treasury
G entrance staircase
H Gate of Xerxes
J *apadana* (throne room)
K council hall
L palace of Darius I
M palace of Xerxes
N palace of Artaxerxes
P harem of Xerxes

Nebuchadnezzar's son and successor, Amel-Marduk (Evil-Merodach, 562–560 BCE), was unable to prevent rivalry between priests and the state from breaking into open disagreement. His brother-in-law Neriglissar (also called Nergal-Ashur-Usur) had him assassinated and seized the throne.

Neriglissar reigned for only four years, apparently dying from natural causes, to be followed by his son Labashi-Marduk. His support of the priests against the army angered his military commanders and he was overthrown and killed in a military coup after only nine months in power.

The military faction placed the elderly Nabonidus (Nabu-Naid, 556–539 BCE) on the throne. However, he raised the status of the Assyrian moon god, Sin, above that of Marduk. The annual New Year ceremonies during which images of Marduk and Nebu were carried in procession through the city did not take place in this period. The priests caused the king to be exiled, leaving Babylon in the charge of his son, the prince-regent Belshazzar (Bel-Shar-Utsur).

Achaemenid Persians

In 539 Cyrus II of the Achaemenid dynasty of Persia defeated the Babylonian army in a battle on the Tigris near present-day Baghdad. Belshazzar was killed and Nabonidus hurried back to Babylon to find Cyrus's army marching unopposed into the city. Cyrus promised to have exiled deities returned and let the Jews return to their homeland, and was welcomed by the city. From this point onward the center of political power shifted from Babylon to Cyrus's capital, first at Pasargadae and then Persepolis. Mesopotamia became merely a large province of the first Persian Empire.

By 486 BCE, under the successors of

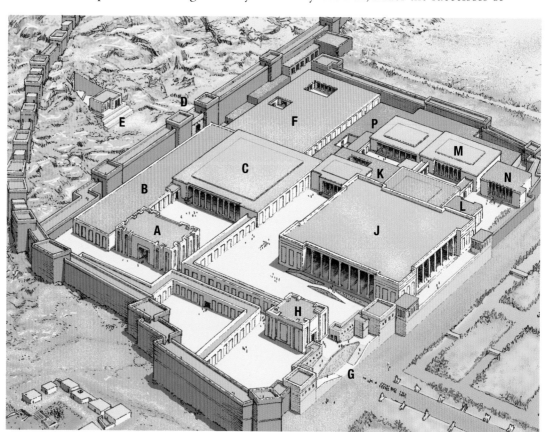

Cyrus, Cambyses II and Darius I the Great, the Achaemenids conquered a territory extending from western India to the edges of Greece, and from southern Russia to all of the eastern North African coast. Darius I famously made war on the Greeks, but failed to win an advantage.

Alexander and the Seleucids

His son Xerxes (486–465 BCE) also launched a campaign against Greece, but similarly failed to defeat the Greeks. From about 965 BCE the Achaemenids' empire was in decline. Its size made it difficult to govern, and the Persians became such unpopular rulers that in 336 BCE Alexander the Great of Macedon, who had united the Greek states, was able to conquer Egypt without resistance. By 330 BCE the whole of the Persian Empire had come under his control.

Following Alexander's death in 323, rule of his empire passed to several of his generals, who fought among each other for total control. The most successful were Ptolemy, who took over Egypt, and Seleucus, who founded the Seleucid dynasty that controlled Mesopotamia.

The Arsacid Parthians

The Seleucid kings soon found themselves under pressure from a group of nomadic people known as the Parthavia, who had moved in 312–261 BCE from central Asia into the region east of the Caspian Sea.

The first chieftain to unite these Parthians was Arsaces I (247–211 BCE). He founded

the Parthian Arsacid dynasty, which went on to sweep away the Seleucids, and build the second Persian Empire. Under the Arsacids the Parthians clashed with the growing Roman Empire on many occasions.

Parthian light cavalrymen were experts at firing over their shoulders in mid-gallop—the "Parthian Shot," from which we derive the phrase "parting shot."

The neo-Persian Sassanids

The continual wars with Rome eventually weakened the Parthians, and the Arsacid dynasty fell to a new Persian power—the Sassanians—in 224 CE. This neo-Persian empire was longer lasting, making war against the Roman and then the Byzantine empires. The Sassanids finally fell before the onslaught of Muslim Arabs in 634 CE, and Mesopotamia became the heartland of a new Islamic dynasty.

Left: Bust of Alexander the Great, who conquered the known world between 336–332 BCE, and founded the Hellenic Seleucid dynasty.

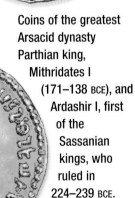

Coins of the greatest Arsacid dynasty Parthian king, Mithridates I (171–138 BCE), and Ardashir I, first of the Sassanian kings, who ruled in 224–239 BCE.

Glossary

Achaemenid A dynasty of ancient Persia, also known as the First Persian Empire. Founded in 539 BCE by Cyrus the Great, son of a minor ruler in Iran named Achaemenes, it is noted for its developments in art and architecture, literature, and for the spread of the *Zoroastrian* religion. The dynasty ended when its last king, Darius III, was defeated by Alexander the Great in 330 BCE.

Akkadian Dynasty founded by Sargon of Agade, who combined Sumer and Akkad to form an early empire. It was overthrown by the *Gutians*. The name also refers to an ancient branch of the *Semitic* languages.

Amorites Old Testament name for the *Elamites*, an ancient people living in Mesopotamia, Syria, and Palestine in the 3rd millennium BCE.

Anu In the Assyrian-Babylonian *pantheon*, the equivalent of the Sumerian god An, though he now becomes the god of kingship as well as that of Heaven.

Anunnaki The four creator gods in Sumerian mythology.

Aqueduct A channel for transporting water which, depending on the terrain, may run along the ground, under it in a pipe, or above it carried on a bridge.

Arab A group of *Semitic* people living in Arabia.

Aramaic A *Semitic* language closely related to *Hebrew*, also known as Aramaean. It was used as the common language in the Near East from 700 BCE and is still spoken in some communities.

Arsacids Dynasty of Parthians founded by Arsaces I in 247 BCE, that lasted through various branches of the family until its defeat by the *Sassanids* in 224 CE. Sometimes referred to as the Parthian Empire.

Aryan Term used to refer to the language or people of the Iranian and Indian branches of the Indo-European group.

Babel Old name for Babylon. Babylon is a Greek rendition of Babel or Bab-ili, meaning the Gate of the God.

Babylonia Region in southern Mesopotamia, referred to in the early period as Sumer. Babylonia was a political entity 1900–1100 BCE, when *Sumer* and *Akkad* were united by the *Amorites*. The name is sometimes used to refer to the Neo-Babylonian, or *Chaldean*, empire of 612–539 BCE.

Chaldean Also referred to as Neo or New Babylonian, 630–539 BCE. In the southern part of Babylonia, it was formed by *Semitic* peoples originating from Arabia who settled in the region c.800.

city-state An independent, self-governing state centered on a single city and its surrounding land.

Code of Hammurabi Set of laws compiled by Hammurabi consisting of 282 provisions and setting out judgments and punishments. The code is the origin of "an eye for an eye, a tooth for a tooth."

cult The worship of a particular god or goddess, or the practice of a particular set of religious rites.

cuneiform Wedge-shaped form of writing and mathematics, widespread in Mesopotamia and Persia, made with a stylus in wet clay and characterized by its straight-edged, block-like form.

dowry The money or property given to a husband by the bride's family when she marries.

dynasty Term used to describe a succession of rulers within a family, usually from father to son. Dynasties are usually referred to by the family name.

Elamites A people from Elam, the land east of the River Tigris. Sargon of Akkad conquered Elam in 2340 BCE.

Gutians A warrior tribe from the Zagros Mountains on the Iran-Iraq border. They invaded the *Akkadian* empire, leading to a period of strife and civil war.

harem Term used to describe the part of a house or palace reserved strictly for women, usually the wives and concubines of a ruler or wealthy noble.

Hebrew Ancient *Semitic* language and people, also the language of the *Israelites* and Jews.

Hittites A major power in Asia Minor (Turkey), 1700–1200 BCE. They conquered northern and central Syria and most of Lebanon, but were eventually absorbed into the Assyrian and Babylonian empires.

Indo-European The name given to those groups of people speaking Indo-European languages who migrated into the Middle East in about 2000 BCE. The languages include Iranian, Armenian and the ancient language of India, Sanskrit.

Israelites   The *Hebrew* inhabitants of the Kingdom of Israel.

Jews   The *Semitic* people who practice the *monotheistic* religion of Judaism, also known as *Hebrews* and *Israelites*.

Kassites   One of the Hurrian tribes from the Zagros Mountains. They overran Babylon in 1595 BCE and formed a loose kingdom c.1570–1160, for a brief period of which Assyria was a vassal state.

Lugal   Sumerian "great man." Originally the name given to a titled landowner, but as their power increased the title became associated with that of the **ensi** (provincial governor) and eventually with that of the king himself.

Medes   Indo-European groups who inhabited the ancient region of Media in modern Azerbaijan, northwest Iran, and northeast Iraq. Between the 7th and 6th centuries BCE they controlled an empire that included most of Iran.

mercenary   A soldier who fights for pay in a foreign army.

Mitanni   One of the Hurrian states that had control over a loose empire c.1550–1370 BCE, and which probably acted as an intermediary between Mesopotamia and Egypt.

Monotheism   The worship of only a single god, such as the *Jews*, in contrast to *polytheism*.

pantheon   Term used to describe all the gods a people worships.

Parthians   See *Arsacids*.

Pathavia   *Achaemenid* spelling for

Parthia, originally part of the Persian Empire.

Persia   Old name for Iran, but also refers to the empire established by the *Achaemenid* dynasty that included parts of Greece and extended into India. The empire was destroyed by Alexander the Great in 330 BCE.

Persis   Old name for *Persia*.

Polytheism   The worship of many gods (deities) within a *pantheon* of deities.

relief   A sculpture carved on a flat background, as opposed to a free-standing sculpture. Raised reliefs (or bas-reliefs) were made by cutting away the background and modeling details onto the figures.

sacrifice   An offering made to a god by a priest or an ordinary person. Offerings were usually gifts of food or flowers, but often included the ritual killing of animals, sometimes even of humans.

Sassanids   Dynasty of Sassanian Persians founded by Sassan, who claimed (almost certainly wrongly) descent from the earlier Persian rulers, the Achaemenids. The Sassanid king Ardashir I overthrew the last *Arsacid* King Artabanus IV in 224 CE to create the Second Persian Empire. Despite much royal infighting between the various branches of the dynasty, the Sassanids lasted until 634 CE, falling to Islamic *Arabs*.

scribe   A person specifically employed to write and copy texts and keep records. In a time when few could read or write, scribes held high status, were well paid, and frequently became powerful men in the state's government.

Scythians   Distant relatives of the *Parthians*. They were responsible for

many of the robberies carried out along the Silk Road trade route during the 1st century BCE.

Sealand   Tribal groups lead by feudal warlords who occupied southern Mesopotamia in the 16th century BCE.

Seleucid   Dynasty and kingdom founded by Alexander the Great's Macedonian general Seleucus Nicator. In 304 BCE the Seleucids seized a large part of Alexander's empire. In 64 BCE Seleucid lands were conquered by the Romans.

Semites   Groups of people who spoke closely related dialects which form part of the language group known as **Semitic**. They occupied an area stretching from northern Mesopotamia to the eastern borders of Egypt. Ancient Semites include the *Hebrews*, *Akkadians* and Babylonians. Arabs and Jews are modern Semites.

Sumerians   Native non-Semitic peoples of ancient Sumer. The word is also used in reference to their language, the oldest known in written form.

tribute   Financial payment as a tax or as a punishment made by a *vassal* to its sovereign power.

vassal   A person or state that is under the control of a more powerful person or state. Vassals are obliged to pay their sovereign *tribute* in goods, soldiers, or money.

ziggurat   A stepped pyramid, usually constructed as the principal building in a Mesopotamian city and dedicated to its patron god.

Zoroastrianism   A faith developed by Zoroaster (or Zathrustra) in Persia c.500 BCE, which became the religion of the Persian Empire.

Index